Understanding IT
A Manager's Guide

Dave Aron and
Jeffrey L. Sampler

PARK LEARNING CENTRE
UNIVERSITY OF GLOUCESTERSHIRE
P.O. Box 220, The Park
Cheltenham GL50 2QF
Tel: 01242 532721

FT **Prentice Hall**
FINANCIAL TIMES

An imprint of **Pearson Education**

Harlow, England • London • New York • Boston • San Francisco • Toronto • Sydney • Singapore • Hong Kong
Tokyo • Seoul • Taipei • New Delhi • Cape Town • Madrid • Mexico City • Amsterdam • Munich • Paris • Milan

Pearson Education Limited
Edinburgh Gate
Harlow
Essex CM20 2JE
England

and Associated Companies throughout the world

Visit us on the World Wide Web at:
www.pearsoneduc.com

First published 2003

British Library Cataloguing-in-Publication Data
A catalogue record for this book is available from the British Library

Library of Congress Cataloging-in-Publication Data
Aron, Dave.
    Understanding IT : a manager's guide / Dave Aron and Jeffrey L. Sampler.
       p. cm.
    Includes bibliographical references and index.
    ISBN 0-273-68208-3 (pbk.)
       1. Information technology–Management. 2. Electronic commerce–Management. 3.
Management information systems. 4. Business enterprises–Communication
systems–Management. 5. Computer networks–Management. I. Sampler, Jeffrey L. II.
Title.

    HD30.2.A76 2003
    004'.068–dc21
                                                                2003042397

10 9 8 7 6 5 4 3 2
08 07 06 05 04 03

Typeset in $10\frac{1}{2}/13\frac{1}{2}$pt Sabon by 35
Printed in Great Britain by Henry Ling Ltd., at the Dorset Press, Dorchester, Dorset

The publisher's policy is to use paper manufactured from sustainable forests.

Everything should be made as simple as possible, but no simpler.

Albert Einstein

Contents

Foreword

As the CEO of Symbian I see many organisations (in the private and public sectors) that are not exploiting existing technologies successfully and that are not aware of emerging technologies that have the potential to transform their industry or sector.

I believe that now, more than ever, general managers must strive to understand technology, in order to ensure that it is well implemented in their organisations, and to inform their corporate strategy. We will continue to see those that succeed in this achieve greater success than those who treat IT as a black box and 'leave it to the IT department'.

This book explains the key IT concepts in clear language, and will be a really useful aid for general managers and business students in understanding the world of IT and its use in business. By training I was not a technologist but have had to acquire my understanding of the IT sector through experience and application.

I wish I'd had this book as the starting point in that process!

David Levin
CEO, Symbian Ltd

Acknowledgements

We would like to thank the faculty and staff of London Business School for the opportunity to expose our material to the critical eye of the MBA class, especially Michael Earl, George Yip, Julia Tyler, and the Class of 2003.

We would also like to thank friends and colleagues in the IT industry, who have helped shape our understanding of that industry over the last 20 years or so, especially Sandro who has defected to the dark side (VC), and Andy who has remained a long-haired techie despite societal, familial, commercial, and sartorial pressures.

The publishers are grateful to the following for permission to reproduce copyright material: Dorling Kindersley, Hewlett-Packard Company, Intel Corporation, Multi-Tech Systems, Inc., 3Com Corporation, Nokia, Compaq, mmO$_2$ plc, NTT DoCoMo, Sony Ericsson, Pogo Technologies and Therefore.

Preface
Why general managers should understand more about IT

Information and communications technologies (ICT) are presenting an unprecedented challenge to markets, investors, and managers, that has resulted in the dot com boom and bust, and many incumbents losing significant share to new players with more sophisticated interweaving of ICT strategy and corporate strategy. (Note that for the rest of this book ICT will be referred to as IT [Information Technology], as this acronym is more widely used.)

More fundamentally, information technology is like fire. It has the power to transform or destroy companies. Much like the promise of any gold rush, this seductive force has the potential for wealth creation that has been the driving force for much of the investment in, and adoption of, technology today.

Indeed, over the last few decades, we have witnessed entire industries transform their basis of competition (such as the airline industry), and companies leading these changes (such as American Airlines and their SABRE reservation system) have often been significant users of information and communications technologies. However, technology fundamentally shifts the capabilities and tools that an organization has at its disposal. The purpose of this book is to help managers 'look under the hood' at the capabilities and forces driving these new technologies. We feel that this is critical to any manager today, as harnessing the power of technology represents one of the most fundamental challenges for current and future business leaders.

However, it is important to understand that IT has not always been the potential wildfire rushing through the dried forest of traditional business models and competitors. IT began as a small spark in most organizations, being used for very technical, mathematically intensive applications, such as calculating rocket trajectories or actuarial tables. In fact, when IBM first introduced mainframe computers into the business world, they believed the market was tiny, because only companies such as very large insurers would be able to derive sufficient value from them.

As the price of technology began to fall, and IT's capabilities increased, it was used for more mainstream number-intensive applications, such as payroll and accounting. In fact, many companies believed that finance and accounting was the sole use of IT, and hence the IT function often reported to the finance or accounting department – a trend which has continued in some companies, but seems more and more inappropriate.

Over time, the use of IT moved from being intra-departmental to interdepartmental (and later between companies), and communications and data storage became key roles of technology. With these changes, companies were able to experiment with different organizational forms, including more extensive outsourcing and delayering management.

With all these changes, business leaders have to face a number of challenges. First, they have to absorb new technologies and understand the new business challenges and opportunities those technologies enable. Secondly, they have to address the IT resources needed to meet those challenges and exploit those opportunities. Thirdly, they have to decide how best to organize the IT function, because of its changing impact and reach within, and outside, their companies. Finally, they are having to address all of these issues in the context of the ongoing, rapid evolution of IT. What was the right answer yesterday is often not the right answer tomorrow.

The challenge to markets and investors

Free markets work best under conditions of balanced liquidity of resources, unobstructed competition, and a high degree of transparency.

IT represents a massive issue in all three of these areas, both in the IT industry and in all other industries. Balanced liquidity of resources means that all resources and structures are able to move at similar speeds, including market structure, capital, skills and skill requirements, corporate strategies, and key success factors. While this ideal is never fully achievable, with the advent of fast-moving IT technologies and products that can turn key success factors and skill needs on their head, market structure cannot keep up.

Further, since IT industry structure is poorly understood and highly fluid, it is tremendously difficult to ensure a competitive playing field and legislate in anti-trust cases. The best example of this is the Microsoft anti-trust court case. It is not difficult to decide whether Microsoft had behaved badly in terms of pressuring PC vendors unfairly to bundle their software with PCs (at least no more difficult than any normal legal case). It seems, however, very difficult for a court to argue credibly whether or not a Web browser (Internet Explorer) should or should not be forcibly bundled with an operating system. It is not that experts are needed to clarify the issue – no-one can clarify the issue, since just what an operating system is is undefined and fast evolving, and it is by no means clear whether a Web browser is tightly integrated with an operating system or not.

Finally, transparency is the worst hit of the three 'capitalist virtues' listed above. IT is extraordinarily complex, extremely fast moving (in terms of raw horsepower of chips, memory and communications media, and also in terms of the sophistication of the software that uses that infrastructure), and unprecedentedly pervasive in terms of the effect it can have on industries and markets.

The challenge to general managers

Similarly for general managers, IT represents a unique challenge. For now and for the foreseeable future, the ways to use IT and the capabilities of IT are changing so fast that IT must always be one of the drivers of corporate strategy, rather than an output of it.

We often see companies failing through designing IT strategies based on corporate strategy (see the Boo.com example in Chapter 1), and conversely we see companies creating supernormal growth through an IT-leveraged corporate strategy (see the Capital One example in Chapter 1). Further, even companies who are not felled by inappropriate IT strategies may be tripped up by poor communication between IT staff and general managers.

All of this is due to the comprehensive impact IT can have on almost any business. IT can affect corporate effectiveness (revenues), efficiency (processes and costs), communications, and decision making (learning and knowledge management).

And the tricky part is that the devil is in the detail. It is almost impossible to abstract successfully from the technical detail, as small technical
issues can invalidate larger strategic plans. Note that many of the business strategy consultancies have found this out to their cost as they have
been largely ineffectual in solving many IT-related issues in their large
corporate clients.

All of this means that general managers cannot devolve and ignore
the details of their IT strategies, but do not know enough about IT to
contribute, and are often afraid of doing so. This fear is sometimes a
key tool of IT staff who thrive, both financially and emotionally, on the
mystique of IT.

The solution – education

The solution is more education for all in information and communications technology concepts. IT needs to be a part of formal primary,
secondary, and tertiary education, and also a part of a businessperson's
armoury of education.

Unfortunately, while there is a great deal of IT training available, it is
seldom of the right sort for the businessperson's needs. It is either nuts
and bolts training in topics such as Microsoft Excel usage, programming
in Java, or Oracle database administration, or it is top level IT strategy
seminars, which skim across the surface, without getting into the sub-
stance of IT.

What is really needed is education for non-technologists in the fundamentals of IT, so that they have the vocabulary to think through the
impact of IT decisions on profitability models, value chain dynamics, etc.

Purpose of the book

This book is motivated by three central tenets:

- IT has had and will continue to have massive impact on the business
  world.
- IT is very complex and difficult to implement well.

■ Significant competitive advantage can be had in corporations, financial institutions, and other professional advisory services, through general managers understanding IT better.

This book is designed to help close the gap between general managers and the world of information technology and technologists. It is primarily a book of concepts, not numbers. It is a book to give the generalist ways of thinking about and understanding IT, not a compendium of facts and figures to use for business planning, nor a guide to programming, or to using a PC.

The target audience includes the board and senior management teams of corporations (CEOs, COOs, CFOs), general managers, MBA students, non-technical management of IT startups, venture capitalists and investment bankers, management consultants, patent agents, accountants, lawyers, human resource managers, and recruitment consultants.

So read this book, and arm yourself with a clear understanding of the most important driver of change in the business world in the last 30 and next 30 years.

Figure P.1 Visual map of the book.

How to use the book

Apart from the Preface and Introduction, each chapter builds on the previous ones, making use of concepts already developed. Hence, by far the best use of the book is to read it in order. Some may find Chapters 1 and 2 too basic, and may wish to begin at Chapter 3 – Software.

Figure P.1 summarizes visually how the chapters of the book fit together to paint the whole picture of the IT world.

Appendix IV contains a brief 'IT literacy test'. It may be interesting to readers to take the test before reading the book, then to review the test after reading the book. Finally, Appendix V contains a list of suggested further reading.

An instructor's manual, PowerPoint slides, Web links and periodical updates are available for lecturers to download at http://www.booksites. net/aron

Introduction
The importance of information technology

Concepts covered in this chapter

■ Definition of the IT industry
■ Size of the IT industry
■ Reasons for managers to understand IT
■ Examples of good and bad use of IT – Capital One and Boo.Com

Questions to ponder before reading

■ Why should a business manager understand IT any more than any
  other specialized technology used in his/her business?
■ How large is the IT industry, in terms of global revenues?

A definition

By information technology, we mean all the hardware, software, and
content technologies that relate to the creation, storage, distribution,
and presentation of digital information.

There are many names for the industry/set of industries and functional disciplines. A few are given in Table 1.1.

Throughout this book, the term IT is used to refer to all technologies
related to the use of digital information. This term was chosen as it is
probably the most familiar to most people, but note that, when some
authors use the term IT, it does not cover communications technologies,
whereas in this book it does.

Table 1.1 Names for the information technology industry.

IT	Information Technology
ICE	Information, Communications, and Electronics
ICT	Information and Communications Technologies
TMT	Telecoms, Media, and Technology
ITT	Information Technology & Telecoms
IS	Information Systems
MIS	Management Information Systems
E-Commerce	Electronic Commerce
M-Commerce	Mobile (or multimodal) Commerce
.com	Internet content based businesses, or high-tech startups in general

Need for managers to understand

A question that one might pose is – why should senior management understand this industry more than any other technology utilized in their business? For example, why should a senior manager in Coca-Cola Corporation understand IT, and not bottling technology? There are at least five reasons:

- IT affects strategy; bottling technology is operational.
- IT can affect many functions; bottling technology has limited functional scope.
- It is clear how to apply bottling technology to the business; applications of IT are unlimited, and hence require a creative combination of corporate visioning and understanding of IT.
- IT has potentially massive leverage (ability to affect profitability), whereas one would expect improvements in bottling technology to affect profitability by at most a couple of percentage points.
- IT can be used to change both revenues and costs, whereas bottling technology (like most other technologies) affects costs primarily.

Thus, IT represents a massive opportunity to almost every business, but is a tremendous challenge to use well.

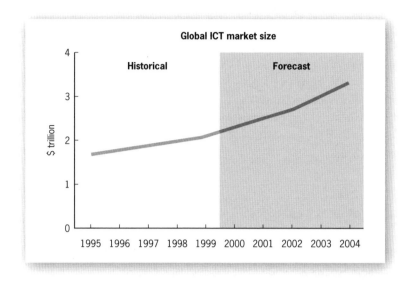

Figure 1.1 The size of the ICT industry. (Source: World Information Technology and Services Alliance (WITSA), source of data International Data Corporation (IDC))

The opportunity of IT

IT pervades most aspects of life in the developed world. Computers can obviously be found in server rooms, call centres, corporate offices, and home offices. But they are also found in videogame consoles, inside cars, embedded in white goods, like washing machines, in televisions and video recorders, and of course inside mobile phones.

Global spending on information and communications technologies markets, including products and services, was over US$2 trillion in 1999, as shown in Figure 1.1. This represented around 4.5% of global GDP. Although the forecast growth in the figure may have changed since the recent dot com crash, it is still true to say that the ICT industries will continue to be important, large, complex, and dynamic, affecting almost every aspect of almost every industry for the next few years.

Current business literature abounds with examples of companies in a wide variety of industries turning their business around, changing business models, or creating structural change in their industry through innovative strategic use of IT. This phenomenon is by no means limited to high-tech firms. Waste Management Inc., a US garbage disposal company, and Cemex, a large cement player, join Cisco in citing sophisticated IT systems as allowing them to consolidate their industries with extensive merger and acquisition (M&A) strategies.

Further, consideration of information technologies and information has made companies rethink their core competencies, and hence what would constitute their most attractive strategic business expansion. Perhaps the clearest case of this is Capital One, as described in the following text box.

Real world example: Capital One[1]

Capital One are one of the clearest examples of success through including a strong understanding of IT in corporate planning.

Starting in 1995, as a spin-off of Signet, a small US bank, Capital One entered the credit card industry – an industry full of strong, entrenched players with deep pockets, trust relationships with customers, and synergistic products – seemingly very high barriers to entry.

Capital One call their strategy an 'information-based' strategy. They felt that entrenched players were segmenting their customer base too crudely, effectively either over- or under-pricing each customer's risk. Capital One believed that, by deploying advanced data mining technologies, they would be able to micro-segment consumer risk, resulting in undercutting competitors for valuable customers, and avoiding taking on loss-making customers.

Results appear to have borne out their approach. Capital One are a top-ten bank card company in the United States, with global revenues of around US$6 billion in 2001, with 44 million customers, and managed loans of $45.3 billion. Capital One's revenues continued to grow quarter by quarter in 2002.

Further, Capital One realized that their major differentiated asset is the understanding of consumer risk, and hence are well poised to enter any market that depends on consumer cash flows over time. So far they have entered the managed loan and car leasing businesses based on their 'information based strategy'.

---

[1] Source: Capital One Website.

The challenge of IT

The problem is that IT does not come with a 'how-to' manual. It is up to every manager to envisage how IT can best be leveraged in their business, then ensure that their IT department and/or their outsourced vendor execute on that vision.

Unfortunately, while there are many success stories, as documented above, the press is also littered with horror stories, of millions of dollars wasted, and corporate focus diverted inwards. Perhaps the most painful example is that of FoxMeyer, a US drug company that at one time had sales of over US$5 billion. A failed implementation of SAP, led by Andersen Consulting (AC – now Accenture), cost them US$30 million, reportedly twice the amount quoted by AC, and could only handle a small fraction of their orders. FoxMeyer ended up spiralling down into bankruptcy, blaming the ERP (Enterprise Resource Planning) installation, and later suing SAP and Andersen for US$500 million each.[2]

Destruction of business value can result from failing to include IT capabilities and constraints in strategic planning, implementing new technology too soon, failing to choose a technology that fits well with business needs, or simply failing to manage the implementation of a critical project.

A good example of the first of these is Boo.com, discussed in the following text box.

Hence, it is of great value to the general manager and student of business to gain a high-level understanding of information technology capabilities and constraints. The next six chapters go on to build up a picture of the current and emerging world of information and communication technologies.

---

[2] Source: Techweb article 'Andersen Sued Over "Flawed" SAP R/3 Job', July 3, 1998, by Bruce Caldwell, *InformationWeek*.

Real world example: Boo.com[3]

Boo.com is an excellent example of a company whose failure to approach IT was a major source of value destruction. Started in 1999, Boo.com was a 'funky' online fashion retailer, delivering fashion shopping over the Internet with a highly rich multimedia experience. Based on the bullish market, and the founders' skills, they were able to raise an amazing US$135 million. Backers included Goldman Sachs and J.P. Morgan.

By mid-2000, it was all over, with most of that money wasted, with only a tiny residual value achieved through selling the brand and other assets. Industry experts estimate that US$120 million was burned in six months, suggesting a quarterly burn rate of US$60 million. Their final quarter's sales were $0.7 million.

There was US$0.5 million in the bank at the time of closure. Brightstation bought the technology for less than US$0.5 million. Fashionmall.com bought the brand and content for an undisclosed amount.

It is arguable whether the IT mistakes they made were the most important, as other significant errors included over-marketing, an unworkable refunds policy, being globally distributed from the start, and possibly failing to understand their target market. A further problem was a five-month delay in launch.

A key IT mistake was to deliver an offering with a very rich user interface that required high-speed Internet access, when at the time almost no-one had it – 8% of US users and 1% of UK users had broadband at the time.

This sounds like a simple error, but fundamentally it came from ignoring IT considerations at the senior management/strategic level. Neither founder had experience or interest in technology, and former IT staff's opinions can be found on various Internet sites complaining bitterly about no-one listening. (Perhaps IT staff always say that anyway!)

Cofounder Ernst Malmsten was quoted at the time of the collapse as saying 'We have been too visionary.'

A good lesson in not considering IT a given in strategic planning.

---

[3] Sources: *Ecommerce Times* ('Ten Worst Dot-Coms Show How Bad Ideas Fed the Web Bust', L.A. Lorek, May 20, 2002), *Industry Standard* ('Boo.com: Better to Come Back Than to Fade Away?', October 12, 2000), *Red Herring* ('The Red Eye: Dot-commers in the UK', Tony Perkins, May 31, 2000), *TNL.Net* ('Boo.Com Goes Bust', May 19, 2000), *BBC.Com* ('Top web retailer collapses', May 18, 2000).

Management perspectives

Our brief overview of the power of IT clearly shows the potential power of technology to alter a firm's capabilities, as well as shifting the basis of competition within an industry. Therefore, understanding how to harness its strengths is one of the key managerial challenges for leaders of today and tomorrow. The following is a list of issues to consider:

- What aspects of IT are critical in my firm's business model? How well does management understand these critical IT capabilities?
- How are my competitors using IT to enable and support their current business strategy? Is my company ahead of or behind these competitors, with regard to the use of IT?
- What industries or companies are the best references or benchmarks for evolving my firm's use of IT?
- In which areas are we using proven technologies? Where are we incorporating leading edge technologies, and are we using any bleeding edge technologies? Is this an appropriate mix?
- Does my firm have a means of keeping abreast of the changing capabilities of IT? If not, does it need one? If so, is the right amount of resource devoted to it?

CHAPTER

2

What a computer is

A soft machine

A computer is a soft machine. The fundamental difference between a computer and any other machine, such as a car, is that its function can be changed without changing its physical form. A car is a vehicle for moving people and goods from A to B. It may be used for a number of reasons – business travel, logistics, commuting, holidaying – but ultimately it is all about movement.

My Compaq iPAQ PDA, on the other hand, functions as an alarm clock, a phone, a calculator, a diary, a game, a word processor, an expenses recorder, and a voice recorder almost every day for me. This variety of functions is similarly true for the average company's servers – acting as payroll calculator, printing facility, inventory management tool, factory management tool, etc.

A corollary of this 'softness' is that an entrepreneur in a remote country can start a new business tomorrow, and provide software which changes what my computing assets can do.

Ubiquity

In essence, a computer is a machine whose function is defined by information, as opposed to mechanical components. Computers are everywhere. They exist in corporate computers, home PCs, and games consoles. They also exist in home appliances, digital watches, videocameras, and washing machines.

Scope of computers

As shown in Figure 2.1, in general, computers can help businesses in four ways, and consumers in four ways. The corporate taxonomy is as follows:

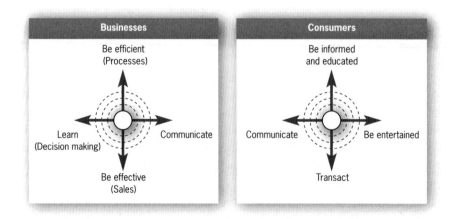

Figure 2.1 The scope of computing.

- Effectiveness – boosting sales through use of the online channel for sales and/or marketing, customer relationship management (CRM) tools to enhance customer acquisition and retention, etc.
- Efficiency – reducing costs through automating and integrating processes.
- Communication and collaboration – online communication and marketplaces help reduce the inefficiencies of legal and cultural boundaries between companies and branches.
- Learning and decision making – data warehousing, data mining, knowledge management, etc., help to capture and use explicit and implicit knowledge, creating a tighter feedback loop.

For consumers, the benefits are as follows:

- Information/education – new ways of getting and sharing information, including more timely news and more interactive educational media.
- Entertainment – different forms of entertainment, including electronic games, view-on-demand movies, online dating, online chat.
- Communication – the ability to communicate with people in more places, in a more timely fashion, or in a more multimedia way, including instant messaging, chat forums, e-mail, and video conferencing.
- Transactions – e-commerce, allowing online banking, online shopping, auctions, etc.

A digital, electromagnetic medium (for now)

All of the above defines what computers do, and why that is valuable. It is all based on the fact that computers are soft, information-centric machines. Currently, computers are all digital, electromagnetic machines also. This may not always be the case (e.g. biological computing, touched on briefly in Chapter 8 as a 'bleeding edge' technology), but for now we are well on the way with digital electromagnetics, so it is appropriate to define it to help with later chapters.

In the context of computing, digital means that everything is stored as discrete values, the predominant version being binary, where everything

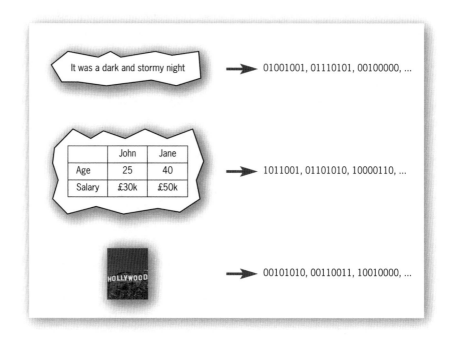

Figure 2.2 The world as '1's and '0's.

is stored as '1's and '0's. Thus, as illustrated in Figure 2.2, a novel, a spreadsheet, a movie, an inventory status report, and a 3D game program are all collapsed to '1's and '0's, which the relevant programs know how to decode as the real world information that they represent.

The reason that computers can do so many things so quickly is precisely because of this. All the lowest level (i.e. the hardware) has to do is shunt '1's and '0's around, and store them.

A single piece of digital information, a '1' or a '0', is called a **bit** (standing for binary digit). For reasons of efficiency, data is normally chunked into groups of eight bits, called one **byte**. One byte can store 2^8 different values = 256 values. Note that sizes of memory and disk storage are normally quoted using multiples of 1000 bytes.[4] See Table 2.1 for the units of memory and storage commonly used.

---

[4] Actually for disks it tends to be multiples of 1000 bytes, for memory it is multiples of 1024 bytes, as 1024 is an exact power of 2. Exact powers of 2 are convenient for computers to handle.

Table 2.1 Units of memory and storage.

Size	Name
1 thousand bytes	1 kilobyte
1 million bytes	1 megabyte
1 billion bytes	1 gigabyte
1 trillion bytes	1 terabyte
10^{15} bytes	1 petabyte
10^{18} bytes	1 exabyte
10^{21} bytes	1 zettabyte
10^{24} bytes	1 yottabyte

For each type of data, there are standards for encoding information into binary. For example, the characters of the English alphabet can be encoded into binary using ASCII (American Standard Code for Information Interchange), where 'Hello' could be represented by the five values 72, 101, 108, 108, 111, or in binary: '01001000', '01100101', '01101100', '01101100', '01101111'.

Standards for graphics include GIF, JPG, BMP, PNG. Standards for movies include MPEG and AVI.

Components

Almost all computers have the following five key components (see also Figure 2.3):

1. A central processing unit (CPU).
2. An input device (such as a keyboard).
3. An output device (such as a screen).
4. Some form of memory to use as working space (also called volatile storage, because its contents are lost when the power is off).
5. Some form of non-volatile storage to remember programs and data files (such as a disk drive).

Whether computers are made of electromagnetic chips, or paper cups and strings, these five components are needed.

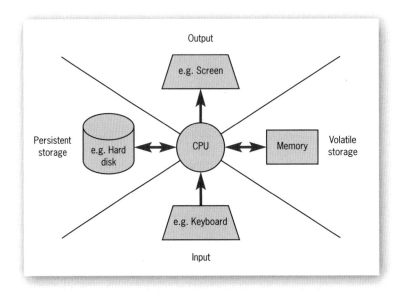

Figure 2.3 The five fundamental components of a computer.

One more key component needed to connect to a network is a modem or network card. A modem handles the process of transmitting a data stream over a telephone line,[5] often between a PC and an Internet service provider (ISP). A network card handles the sending and receiving of packets of information between computers on a network, explained in Chapter 4.

Most real computers have many different input devices (keyboard, mouse, scanner, tablet), many different output devices (screen, printer, fax card), many different forms of volatile and non-volatile storage (memory chip, hard disk, floppy disk, tape, compact flash card), and even several different CPUs (Intel Pentium CPU, graphics chip on graphics card, network logic on Network card).

Fundamentally all the components fall into these six categories (five fundamentals plus network).

---

[5] Similar devices are needed for more modern digital connections that are not telephone lines, e.g. cable networks, but technically they are not modems (which are specifically modulator-demodulator devices for converting between digital and analog signals). However, they continue to be called modems, e.g. cable modems.

Program execution

The only thing that a computer does is execute programs. A program is a set of instructions written in a special language. Almost every CPU understands only one language. This category of languages, which chips understand, is called machine code.

Each CPU (such as a Pentium 3, or a Pentium 4, or a StrongARM) has its own specific machine code, which is usually not the same as any other. However, note that Intel and AMD CPUs have very similar machine codes, required to run the same Windows™ software.

The operations of a computer are synchronized to a clock. The clock generates a periodic 'tick', which signifies the start of each cycle of the computer (see Figure 2.4). For example, if you have a PC with a 1.8 Ghz Pentium chip, there are 1.8 billion cycles per second. Typically, a machine code instruction takes a few cycles to complete, often between 3 and 5. An instruction might involve moving a piece of memory into the CPU for processing, or jumping into a different part of the program.

Instructions are held in memory. The CPU requests the next instruction by putting its address in memory on the address bus. The memory receives the request and puts the instruction on the data bus, which the CPU then receives and executes.

This is the fundamental process of a computer. It is accelerated in most modern systems, like PCs, through the use of caches, which predict which bits of memory might be needed next, and load them into a small piece of memory very close to, or on, the CPU chip.

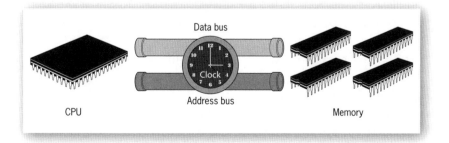

Figure 2.4 A computer's cycle.

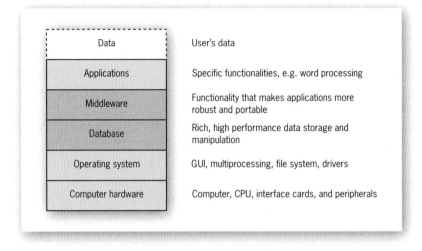

Figure 2.5 The five layers of a computer.

Layers

Computer systems can be thought of as having the following five layers for processing data (see also Figure 2.5):

- The hardware layer, where components are assembled to run machine code programs.
- The operating systems layer, where the operating system, a large machine code program, provides functions that applications need to run, such as a graphical user interface (like Windows™), multiprocessing (the ability for several programs to run at the same time), a file system and drivers for peripherals, such as printers, making them easier to use.
- The database layer, which provides the ability to store large amounts of data, and provides complex data analysis capabilities in an efficient manner.
- A middleware layer, which provides richer functionality than the operating system, but similarly provides services to applications that make it easier to write applications. This may be anything from broad horizontal middleware, such as an application server which

provides robustness and scaling services, to vertical middleware to support a specific functionality, like the sending and receiving of SMS messages over a GSM mobile phone network.

■ An application layer, where specific applications, such as word processors, or ERP systems, reside.

Note that most PCs have hardware, operating system, and applications layers. Database and middleware layers are installed only where needed, typically on server computers.

Companies that make hardware components include Intel, AMD, ARM, and Transmeta (who all make CPU chips – see text box on Transmeta), Creative Labs and Turtle Beach (who make sound subsystems), Nvidia (who make graphics subsystems), and EMC, Western Digital,

Key industry player: Transmeta

Founded in 1995 by David Ditzel from Sun and AT&T, Transmeta represent a potentially significant disruptive force in the CPU and mobile computing hardware world. Transmeta's first chip, the Crusoe, is based on an innovative design, which reduces the number of transistors in the chip, and adds an extra software layer, which provides the complexity missing in the hardware.

A key benefit of this approach is that the CPU is less power hungry, and hence less of a drain on the battery. Further, the Crusoe is able to emulate other chips, notably Intel chips, and also it is able to tune its behaviour by modifying the software layer, by observing how it is being used.

Transmeta have had some early successes, as Japanese laptop manufacturers such as Sony, Toshiba, and Fujitsu have used the Crusoe in their laptops, in order to prolong battery life – one of the key selling points of laptops.

Transmeta have created a genuinely innovative technology, and after IPO in late 2000 have moved from highly innovative R&D mode to strong, commercial delivery. The challenge is now to reach profitability. In 2001, revenues were US$36 million, R&D spend was US$68 million, and net losses were around $171m.

Also of note is that Linus Torvalds, Linux pioneer, is on the staff at Transmeta.

Quantum, and Seagate (who make storage subsystems). Transmeta are an interesting, innovative player, discussed in the text box.

Companies that put together computer hardware based on these components include PC manufacturers such as Dell, Compaq, Sony, Fujitsu, HP, and companies who make Unix workstations such as Sun, and makers of mainframes such as IBM.

The dominant operating system player is Microsoft with its various 'flavours' of Windows™ (NT, 95, 98, 2000, XP). Other players include Sun, who make the Solaris operating system (a type of Unix), and the Open Source movement, who have created Linux and BSD Unix.

The most common database systems are relational database management systems (RDBMS), which refers to the way in which they store and allow linking of data. The key vendors here are Oracle, IBM (DB2 product), Microsoft, Informix, and Sybase.

Middleware is a vast area, but in the application server field (one type of middleware popular with e-commerce applications), key players include BEA, iPlanet, and IBM.

The application area is almost impossible to define, including every maker of almost every type of program, but in the office automation area (word processing, spreadsheeting, etc.) Microsoft is by far the dominant force, with Lotus (now owned by IBM) and various Open Source products (such as StarOffice – now owned by Sun) the major alternatives.

Management perspectives

Having gained an understanding of the components of computer systems, how should managers use this information? The following is a list of issues to consider:

■ Given Moore's Law and the rate of advancement in the capabilities of hardware and the simultaneous decrease in prices, how often should we buy new hardware? Should we buy the latest models as soon as they appear, or go for deep discounts late in a product's fairly short lifecycle?
■ Will the computing power of hardware give my firm a competitive advantage or will it be a competitive necessity? Realize the enormous amounts of money that must be spent to stay ahead in the hardware arena.

- What applications will be possible when hardware is twice as fast (or economically viable when twice as cheap), i.e. in approximately 18 months?
- Will improvements in the price/performance ratio in computer hardware change economies of scale or other aspects of the cost base of competition present in the industry today?
- How much is my firm using IT to ehance effectiveness, efficiency, communication, and learning? Is this mix appropriate? Is too much being focused on any one area? Are any opportunities being left 'on the table'?

CHAPTER

3

How software works

Concepts covered in this chapter

■ Definition of software
■ The thirteen goals of an IT system
■ Types of computer language, and benefits of each type, including object-oriented systems and Java
■ Description of leading ERP software company SAP, and software development in a small mobile Internet startup, xtempus

Questions to ponder before reading

■ What is computer software?
■ Which computer languages do you know? What is the difference between them?
■ What does object-oriented mean?
■ What is so important about Java?
■ When you specify what you want from a computer system, other than specifying what functions it performs for the user, which other characteristics need to be defined?

While hardware and communication links are important parts of an IT solution, being the infrastructure platform, one could argue that software is where the real end-user value is created. A good analogy is of hardware and communications being the roads, and software being the car that you drive down the roads to get to your destination.

What is software?

Software refers to the programs written to run on a computer. Software is written in a particular computer language. Examples of computer languages include 80 × 86 machine code, C, C++, Cobol, Visual Basic, Java.

A computer program is a list of instructions in a particular language, which when executed results in the behaviour desired by the user (e.g. show an account balance, calculate commission, simulate a spaceship travelling through a meteor shower).

The key feature of computer languages is that they are *unambiguous*. Human languages, such as English, are ambiguous, in that many words and phrases have multiple meanings based on the *a priori* experiences of the participants in a communication, for example 'I love you' or 'a lot of money'.

A computer language is very limited, in comparison, but there is no doubt what an instruction means; hence the meaning of a computer program lies entirely within that program, and as such can be processed, propagated around an electronic network, and executed, without reference to any contextual information, such as what the programmer was thinking when he or she wrote the program.

Typically the four types of instruction that a computer language must have are:

- Input/output – including printing to the screen and receiving keyboard input.
- Flow control (including logical conditions) – so that different inputs can result in different program execution.
- Data manipulation – including mathematical operations (such as logarithms) and textual operations (such as concatenation).
- Data movement – so that pieces of information can be moved between memory, screen, and disk, for example.

A very simple example of a program is shown in Figure 3.1.

```
            Input Height;
            Input Weight;
            Density = Weight/Height;
            If (Density > 3) goto BIG;
            If (Density < 2) goto SMALL;
            Output "You're OK";
            Exit;
BIG:        Output "You're too fat";
            Exit;
SMALL:      Output "You're too skinny";
            Exit;
```

Figure 3.1 A simple computer program.

Table 3.1 The thirteen goals of an IT system. (Source: D. Aron)

Functionality	Tasks that system can perform
Cost	Total cost of ownership of system
Performance	Volume of transactions that system can support
Usability	Nature of the user experience
Integrity	Surety that the data in the system will not get lost or corrupted
Security	Surety that people can only access the data they are entitled to
Development speed	The speed with which a system can be developed and delivered
Flexibility	Ability for system to be changed as requirements change
Extensibility	Ability for system to be extended to perform further tasks
Scalability	Ability for system to scale to handle much greater volumes
Robustness	Level of 'uptime' that can be guaranteed
Portability	Ability for system to be implemented on different hardware/ operating systems/databases etc.

The goals of an IT system

In this chapter, we will be discussing different computer languages, and their relative merits. In order to do so, we have first to introduce a framework for evaluating an IT solution. The following thirteen dimensions, or characteristics, define how valuable an IT solution is (see also Table 3.1):

1. **Functionality**. The tasks that the system can perform. For an online banking system, this means 'allowing the user to check their balance', 'allowing the user to transfer funds', etc.
2. **Cost**. The total cost of ownership of the solution, including initial hardware and software purchases, ongoing operating services, cost of maintenance, cost of upgrade, etc.
3. **Performance**. The volume of transactions/users that can be handled by a given installation of the solution. For an online banking system, an appropriate performance metric may be the number of banking transactions that can happen concurrently while maintaining a 4-second response time.
4. **Usability**. The user-friendliness of the solution. Usually the best measure of this is a user survey. Usability can be enhanced by techniques such as JAD (Joint Application Development), where users are involved in the design process.
5. **Integrity**. The certainty that the data in the system will not become corrupted or lost. Ways of ensuring integrity include use of highly available storage systems, comprehensive backups, and implementing rollback/rollforward mechanisms to allow transactions to be undone/redone.
6. **Security**. Ensuring that everyone has an appropriate level of access to the system, allowing people to access what they should be able to, not access what they should not be able to, and not be able to disrupt the access of others.
7. **Development speed**. How quickly the system can be developed. Technologies that help here include rapid prototyping tools, test robots, and automatic documentation generation.
8. **Maintainability**. The effort required to keep the system going. Normally, a certain amount of effort has to be allocated just to keep the system in full working order.
9. **Flexibility**. The effort required to change the system. This requires envisaging the likely changes that might be needed to the system, then estimating the effort required for those changes. An example of a change to an online banking system might be changing transaction dates from two to four figures to accommodate post-year-2000 dates (known colloquially as Y2K).
10. **Extensibility**. Similar to Flexibility, this refers to the effort required to add functionality to a system. In an online banking scenario, this might include adding a loan application function to a basic banking system.

11. **Scalability**. The ease with which system performance can be increased. With a well architected system, it should be possible simply to add extra server computers to a system in order to scale the performance, without adding significant overhead. In other words, ideally scalability should be fairly linear with cost. Practically, achieving completely smooth scalability is very difficult.

12. **Robustness**. The ability for the system to stay up, no matter what happens. The measure of robustness is availability (AKA uptime), and, as computers converge with telecomms, people often talk about computer systems needing to achieve 'five nines' availability, or 99.999%. Mechanisms for achieving robustness centre around removing 'single points of failure', i.e. components whose failure would bring the entire solution down. Technologies include use of highly available storage media, such as mirrored disks, clustering of multiple servers with failover (if one computer fails, another takes over its work), and a good data backup regime.

13. **Portability**. The ability for a solution to be executed on different systems. This is clearly very important for the client part of a business-to-consumer (B2C) e-commerce solution, which should work across as many client systems as possible, e.g. PC, Mac, PDA, WAP phone, i-Mode phone, Linux machine.

Machine code is tough

The most basic computer language is machine code. All that a CPU chip understands is machine code. The good thing about machine code is that it is blindingly fast. As stated above, modern PCs can execute several hundred million instructions per second. The bad thing about machine code is that it is so detailed, in that each instruction does one tiny operation (like moving a number into a byte of memory), therefore it is very difficult to use machine code to write a program of any size or complexity. Figure 3.2 shows an indicative machine code fragment to print the word 'Hello' on the screen, and, to the right of it, the equivalent code in the Basic language.

Not surprisingly, nowadays most large projects are not undertaken in machine code. The only programs typically written in machine code are small, very time critical programs, such as printer drivers, which are required to respond to signals from the printer in a very timely fashion.

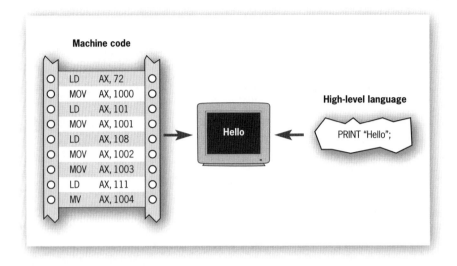

Figure 3.2 Machine code is tough! (Source: D. Aron)

High-level languages

The alternatives to machine code are called high-level languages. They are called high level because they are supposed to be closer to the language of humans and further from the heart of the computer. Every computer language other than machine code[6] is a high-level language. Examples you may have heard of include (Visual) Basic, C, (Visual) C++, SQL, C#, Cobol, Fortran, Java, Javascript, Lisp, and Perl.

All of these languages are much more easily understandable to a human than machine code, but none of them is understandable by a CPU chip. Hence programs written in high-level languages need to be converted to machine code.

There are three methods currently used for this conversion: **compilation, interpretation,** and **intermediate languages,** as shown in Figure 3.3.

A compiler is itself a machine code program. A compiler takes as its input a program in a high-level language, and outputs a machine code program that behaves in the way intended in the high-level program. The resultant machine code program can then be executed on a computer that contains the right type of CPU (e.g. a Pentium® 4 chip).

---

[6] Note that assembly language is an alternative way of displaying machine code, and hence is the only other non-high-level language.

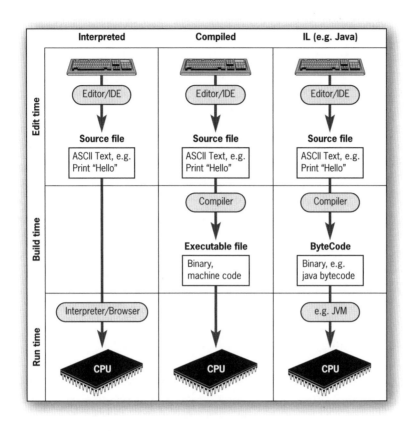

Figure 3.3 The three types of high-level language.

The advantage of using a compiler is that the resulting programs are relatively fast because they are machine code, and they can be run on any computer that has the appropriate CPU type. Another advantage of using a compiler is that a producer of software never has to distribute their source code, which is their intellectual property, to users, but only the machine code executable.

The disadvantage of using a compiler is that the resulting program is not portable to computers with different CPU types. So, for example, if a portal was creating a chat client, which users could download, then use to chat, a compiled program would work on only one type of computer, such as a PC, and not Macintoshes, PocketPCs, or WAP phones. Using the compiler paradigm, the portal company would have to maintain several machine code programs (also called executables) for all the platforms it wanted to support. C++ and Cobol are most commonly implemented as compiled languages.

The alternative to a compiler is an interpreter. An interpreter runs on the target computer, allows the programmer to load the program, and executes it, one instruction at a time, converting each instruction to machine code before executing it. A good analogy is of human translators and interpreters. Typically, a human translator receives a written communication in the source language, and returns a written communication in the target language. In contrast, the human interpreter is present at the time of communication, and translates, sentence by sentence, between the two parties.

The upside of interpreters, compared with compilers, is that the program can be distributed to any computer that has an interpreter for the language, and should run unmodified on that platform. Also, interpreted programs can be run as soon as they are written, without going through a compilation phase.

The downside of interpreters is that interpreted programs tend to execute more slowly (as they are being converted into machine code while running), and an interpreter is required by anyone who wants to run the program.

A common interpreted language at present is Javascript, which may be embedded in Web pages in order to provide rich functionality, such as drop-down menu boxes. In the case of Javascript, the interpreter is part of most Web browsers (e.g. Internet Explorer, Netscape Navigator), which almost every Internet-connected computer includes.

Note that there is also a class of languages, called scripting languages, that tend to be interpreted. These languages include DCL, Perl, and Python. They are typically used to create small programs for administering systems, such as running backups to tape, and the lack of a compilation phase is attractive.

The third fundamental approach to processing high-level languages was pioneered by Sun with the Java language. This attempted to approach the speeds of compiled code while maintaining the portability of interpreted code, which was extremely important as the Web was taking off. The solution is the use of an intermediate language (IL) that is very close to machine code, but is not the same as any one machine code.

In the IL paradigm, source code (e.g. Java) is compiled to an intermediate language called Bytecode, then distributed to any computer wishing to execute it. These computers must have a small program, called a JVM (Java Virtual Machine), that is able to interpret Java Bytecode. Nowadays, most Web browsers contain a Java Virtual Machine. Further, there are mini-JVMs available for phones and embedded processors.

Because intermediate languages are very close to machine code, the interpreting of Bytecode is much faster than conventional interpreting, and hence the execution of Java applets is fast. Also, because IL code is typically much smaller than source code, downloading of 'applets' is much faster than downloading source code. Note that the term 'applet' is the term used for small applications, compiled into Bytecode, to be downloaded, executed, and often subsequently discarded, by the client computer.

This is why Java has proliferated as the language of the Web. Arguably, the other reason is that Sun have been very open with their Java business model, allowing a community of developers to flourish. More recently, Sun have tuned the Java approach to include 'Just In Time' (JIT) compilation, where a downloaded applet is compiled to machine code just before being run, to further improve performance. Recently, Microsoft's C# has appeared as part of their .NET initiative, also using an intermediate language approach.

A comparison of current computer languages

We are now in a position to compare current computer languages, and their efficacy with respect to the thirteen dimensions of IT solution value outlined earlier.

On the left in Figure 3.4 is machine code. The main benefit of machine code as a programming language is its blistering execution speed. However, it is weak on all other dimensions: development is slow, and, because programs end up being long, obscure strings of 'spaghetti code', it is hard to maintain, change, or extend machine code programs. Further, machine code programs are in no way portable, as they are designed to run on only one specific CPU. Lastly, there are also no mechanisms in the language to help with data integrity, scaling across multiple machines, or robustness (removing single points of failure), so the programmer has to do all that work him- or herself. Note that the term 'assembler' is used in Figure 3.4. Assembler is a way of representing machine code (represented by binary numbers) with alphanumeric codes, which are easier for humans to understand, but is otherwise identical to machine code.

The first real improvement was the introduction of 'imperative' high-level languages. Basic, Cobol, and Fortran are examples of an imperative high-level language. The chief benefit of these languages is that they are

Category	Machine code/ Assembler	Imperative	Procedural/ Functional	Object-oriented	'Intermediate'	
Examples	80×86	Basic	C	C++	Java, C#	J2EE, EJB, Corba, .NET
Key benefits	Execution speed	Devt speed	Maintainability	Flexibility Extensibility	Data integrity, Portability	Scalability, Robustness
Key issues	Devt speed, Maintainability, Flexibility, Extensibility, Data integrity, Portability, Scalability, Robustness	Maintainability, Flexibility, Extensibility, Data integrity, Portability, Scalability, Robustness	Flexibility, Extensibility, Data integrity, Portability, Scalability, Robustness	Data integrity, Portability, Scalability, Robustness	Scalability, Robustness	Cost

Figure 3.4 Benefits of different programming languages.

much faster to develop in, as they are much more intuitive and high-level than machine code. High-level languages like these have been in common use commercially since the 1970s.[7]

The next major step was the introduction of procedural and functional languages, such as C and Pascal. The chief benefit of these languages is that specific parts of functionality (e.g. the deposit function in an online banking application) can be encapsulated in a function, so that, if there is a problem with that functionality, maintenance efforts can be focused on the function, which is generally much smaller than the whole program. As a result, maintainability is much better than with machine code.

A very significant step came next – object orientation. Until object orientation, programs were essentially recipes – long lists of instructions that operate on data, in order to produce the desired result. In object-oriented paradigm, information comes to the fore. Programs are collections of objects, with methods that operate on the objects. An object-oriented programming paradigm involves modelling the real world objects that you are trying to emulate with computational objects. In the case of online banking, objects would be created to emulate customers and accounts. Among the benefits of object orientation is the fact that it tends to be cheaper and easier to change or extend object-oriented code – a small change in the real world requirement tends to require only a small change in the corresponding computational objects. Although object orientation has existed in academic circles since the 1960s, it has only been popular commercially since the mid-1990s. The first popular object-oriented language was C++. Others include Java and C#. Also, many implementations of traditional programming languages, like Microsoft Visual Basic, now incorporate many object-oriented features.

As explained in the previous section, Java introduced the concept of the intermediate language, which allowed the creation of much more portable programs. Also, by being more strictly object-oriented than C++, Java improved data integrity capabilities, as all information in a Java program is encapsulated within objects. In general, Java results in faster development and more portable code than C++. However, a common observation is that C++ results in faster code than Java, but with

---

[7] Rather amusingly, when these languages were introduced, some optimists claimed that they were so easy to use that programmers would no longer be necessary. Needless to say, this did not prove correct.

improvements in Java architectures, including JIT compilers (mentioned earlier), this is less of an issue. C# is the other language that supports the intermediate language paradigm at present.

The most recent extension to the computer programming paradigm involves the provision of architectural frameworks containing comprehensive suites of libraries and middleware to accelerate and simplify the development of robust, scalable Web services, with support for lots of functions common to all services, including authentication. The Sun/ Java version of this paradigm includes J2EE (Java 2 Enterprise Edition),

Key industry player: SAP

Formed in 1972 and floated in 1988, SAP AG have become one of the most important players in the IT world. With their mySAP e-business platform, they are the leading Enterprise Resource Planning (ERP) provider with 2001 revenues of €7.3 billion. SAP have also provided massive revenues for the large system integration consultancies like Accenture and KPMG.

For many years all the corporate information systems such as payroll and human resources (HR), inventory and supply chain management, accounting and finance, procurement and decision support were independent of one another, and integration was a difficult task. The Enterprise Resource Planning (ERP) category appeared, with companies recognizing that there were large benefits from driving every business process from an integrated operational database.

Generally, an implementation of a major ERP system takes 12–18 months from start to finish, many taking much longer. Often, ERP implementations accompany Business Process Re-engineering exercises.

SAP are joined by Peoplesoft, JD Edwards, Oracle, and Baan as the top flight of ERP vendors. Technology and commercial challenges that these companies have been facing include responding to the proliferation of the Internet and e-commerce, and managing interoperability between products.

SAP made two key strategic moves in 2000. It created SAP Hosting to exploit the Application Service Provider (ASP) market, and SAP Markets to focus on business-to-business (B2B) marketplaces. More recently, SAP Markets and SAP Portals (focusing on integrated corporate portals) were re-integrated into the core of SAP.

J2ME (Java 2 Micro Edition), and ONE (Open Network Environment). The Microsoft version of this Web services technology is called .NET.

Finally, in the following text boxes we present an example of one of the most successful application software companies to date, SAP, and a real world development technology decision, at xtempus.

Management perspectives

Software is often the most visible interaction point with information technology for the typical manager. This familiarity and the ease of use of much of today's software may actually mask the complexity of issues in this area. Key considerations for managers include the following:

- Of the thirteen goals for an IT system described in this chapter, which are most important to my current business and its competitive strategy? Is my IT team allocating the right amount of resource to each one? Typically, IT departments focus on functionality as it is a very visible dimension, but other dimensions, like robustness, often receive disproportionately little resource.
- Is my IT department making software choices based on rational cost/benefit analysis, or personal preference? Most companies suffer to some extent from IT department biases – as the saying goes, 'If the only tool you have is a hammer, every problem looks like a nail.'
- For my business, what is the balance between striving to implement one great integrated corporate software platform versus small, functional components that are glued together?
- How important is software compatibility across the entire business versus letting separate business units pursue options that may solve local needs better?
- Is software system compatibility a risk criterion or consideration in business acquisitions?
- What are the current software platforms, standards, and trends in the industry today, and is my company compatible with them? Is there any trend emerging that will put my company in an unfavourable cost position, lock us out of opportunities etc.? (At the time of writing, .NET and Web services are interesting trends in this category for many companies.)

Real world example: xtempus software development

When Dave (co-author) became CTO of xtempus in early 2000, the company was only three months old. Although we did not know it then, we were at the tail-end of the dot com boom, and the pressure was on to get going, get products, get customers, and get floated as soon as possible. As we hired people as fast as we could, there was talk of valuation being US$1 million per person – a compelling reason to hire.

The hot topic of the day was mobile Internet, especially WAP. The early team had very quickly built prototypes, using Microsoft technologies, an SQL*Server database with proprietary data structures, and C++. The prototypes were of various mobile Internet applications, including the ability for the operator to set up the user's phone to point automatically to their WAP service without the user having to fiddle around with WAP settings. We gained early interest from many large companies including mobile network operators and consultancies interested in developing mobile services.

Strategically, it began to seem as if, rather than developing applications for mobile phones, we should be developing tools that our customers could use. As that realization dawned on us, it also became clear that C++ and the Microsoft technologies were probably the wrong choice; rightly or wrongly (Dave believed rightly) many of the serious consultancies regarded the Java 2 Enterprise Edition, with Oracle as the database, and XML as the content format, as the right choice for building scalable solutions. Dave chose to switch xtempus technology to J2EE, XML, and a standard database approach that worked with Oracle, consistent with our emerging business model.

It was a tough decision, as the developers we had employed (mostly as contractors) were mainly skilled in Microsoft technologies, not J2EE. It would also inevitably slow us up as we reworked code in J2EE. There was also some doubt as to whether Java would be fast enough for some applications.

By mid-2000, almost everything was in Java, and this decision seemed to win us respect, and get us through the first technology hurdles with consultancies we talked to. This is a good example of technology choices being linked to strategic decisions.

Sad to note, however, other competitors moved quite fast, WAP never really materialized as expected, and at the time of writing xtempus struggles on with a much smaller workforce.

The role of networks and the Internet

Concepts covered in this chapter

- The purpose of computer networks
- Circuit versus packet switching
- The layers of a network
- Different types of network, including LAN, WAN, PAN, WLAN, and WISP
- Examples: WLAN player Mobilestar and Starbucks WLAN service
- Components of the Internet
- Description of network hardware company 3Com, and network software company Citrix

Questions to ponder before reading

- What is a computer network for?
- What different types of computer network are there?
- What are the key components of the Internet, and what are they for?

So far, we have discussed the creation of programs running on computers. Now we will extend this to consider networks.

The purpose of networks

A network allows:

- sharing of data;
- sharing of resources (storage, printers, tapes);
- communication (e.g. e-mail, chat, net meetings, shared whiteboards, video conferencing);

- centralized management (backups, performance monitoring, security enforcement);
- sharing of applications and distributed processing, allowing several computers to share the load of running a computationally intensive application.

As computers have moved from being isolated 'glorified calculators' through to being stations on a corporate network, through to portals into the World Wide Web (WWW), their value and capabilities have increased exponentially.

Bob Metcalfe, one of the creators of Ethernet and one of the founders of the networking company 3Com, stated that the value of a network is proportional to the square of the number of nodes in the network. This statement is known as Metcalfe's Law, and reflects the fact that the cost of adding a node is relatively flat, but the value increases much faster, since, by adding the '$n+1$'th computer to a network, one creates n new links.

Networks for distributed processing

A software solution, whether it is a word processor, a call centre management system, or an online auction, can be run 'standalone' on one computer, or 'distributed' across several computers.

The benefits of standalone processing are simplicity and predictability. There are no issues with the performance of shared resources, like networks, or complications when, for example, one computer crashes while in the middle of processing a transaction. The benefits of distributed processing, on the other hand, include performance and reliability. A properly architected distributed solution can take advantage of the CPUs of each computer, and ensure that, if one computer fails, another takes up the load. In simple terms, if a computer is 80% reliable (i.e. a one in five chance of crashing), a well architected solution using two computers might be 96% reliable, a three-computer solution might be over 99% reliable, and so on.

Distributed processing is either peer-to-peer or client–server. Peer-to-peer architectures are normally used to share the load between servers. Technologies used to synchronize activities between servers include application servers, made by companies such as BEA, object request brokers (ORBs) using standards such as CORBA (Common Object Request Broker Architecture) and IIOP (Internet Inter-ORB Protocol), and queueing mechanisms, such as IBM's MQ-Series.

Client–server architectures are particularly useful when there are many clients, for example a Web-based service. Running everything on a server in such a situation creates a bottleneck at the server. So, the upside of client–server is better performance, but the downside is more complex management. If part of a solution sits on a thousand client computers, upgrades are a nightmare. An effective solution to this problem is 'applets'. Applets are designed to run on the client computer, but sit on the server, and are downloaded to the client computer when it is time for them to run.

Note that in this context a client device could be any device with a processor in it, including a PC, a PDA, a mobile phone, or a vehicle's embedded systems.

Client–server architectures typically distinguish between 'thin client' and 'fat client'. Thin-client solutions perform only very straightforward processing on the client computer, usually related to the graphical presentation of information to the user. Fat-client solutions take much greater advantage of the client CPU, running significant sections of the solution on the client. The challenge with fat-client solutions is that the client device becomes key to maintaining system integrity. If the client device crashes or corrupts data, this can compromise the integrity/experience of many users.

A specialized variant of the fat-client architecture is ICA, or Intermittently Connected Architecture. ICA-architected solutions are designed with the wireless mobile device in mind, where the intention is to reap the benefits of a client–server solution (high-speed number crunching, higher reliability, shared data), but allowing the mobile user to continue working even when the client device becomes temporarily disconnected from the server/network. This is particularly important in a wide area wireless context (e.g. mobile telephony), as connections are frequently unreliable.

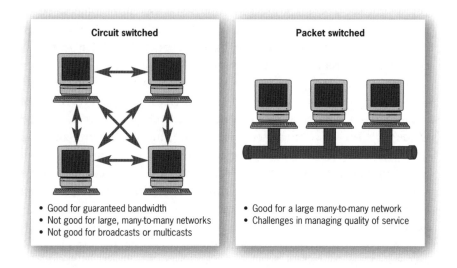

Figure 4.1 Circuit vs packet-switched networks.

How networks work

Communication between two computers requires them to be connected. A simple way of achieving this for many computers is the circuit-switched network, where a physical (e.g. electrical) circuit is established between each pair of computers that wish to communicate. This method ends up being slow and cumbersome, and not very well suited to requirements such as broadcasting messages to all computers on a network. The best alternative is a 'packet switched' network. Figure 4.1 summarizes these two alternatives.

In a packet switched network, rather than have specific computers/ peripherals connect to specific others, each device on the network (often called a node) is connected to a shared 'information highway', and places packets of information on it identifying who it is from and who it is for (also called meta-information).

The benefit of a packet switched network is that it is much cheaper to add a node to it, as the cost function is linear – it is roughly as cheap to add the 1000th node as it is to add the first.

The downside of packet switched networks is that performance is difficult to control. When you have a dedicated link between two computers, you can guarantee what bandwidth is available for communications, e.g. 56 kbps (kbps means thousands of bits per second). With a packet switched network, all participants share the same bandwidth, and hence the performance degrades as the number of 'conversations' over the network increases.

Not only does performance degrade, but it degrades in a dynamic, unpredictable way as no one computer is in control of how many conversations take place at any one time. This problem is referred to as the 'Quality of Service' (QoS) problem, and many companies and consortia are constantly working on solutions in order to allow real-time communications (such as video streaming and voice calls – called VOIP) to work well on a packet switched network.

As will be explained shortly, the shared 'information highway' takes the form of a series of boxes, called hubs, switches, and routers. By using intelligent filtering techniques, it is possible to mitigate some of the above problems.

Despite the QoS drawback, almost every computer network uses a packet switched approach nowadays.

Layers of a network

Since computing is so complex, almost everything is implemented in layers, such that the lower layers implement the detailed things, presenting a simpler interface to the higher layers, allowing them to focus on more user/application oriented problems. This approach (technically called metalinguistic abstraction) has the obvious benefit of simplifying the development of solutions, and also has the benefit of portability. If an application does not refer specifically to an operating system (such as Windows 2000™), or a network protocol (like TCP/IP), but instead refers to abstract functions, such as opening a file, or sending a packet, it is easy to slide in a different operating system or network protocol underneath the application.

We saw this type of layering in Chapter 2, where it was shown how a computer could be split into five layers. Similarly, network communications are split in this way, and the alphabet soup of terms that you might have come across, such as ISDN, ADSL, HTTP, TCP/IP and Ethernet, exists at different layers. There are a number ways to split networks up,

Table 4.1 Conceptual layers of a network.

Layer	Purpose	Components/Term
Networked applications	Applications that run across a network, such as e-mail and Web browsers	Browsers, HTML, e-mail
Session management	Managing lengthy sessions, e.g. sending an e-mail, using many packets	HTTP, FTP, SMTP
Packets and addresses	Addressing mechanism, data split into packets	TCP/IP, DNS, DHCP, NAT
Physical (cables etc.)	Achieve physical connection, low-level addressing	Ethernet, hubs, switches, routers, modems, ISDN, ADSL, SDSL

the most formal being the International Standards Organization's (ISO) Open Systems Interconnect (OSI) seven-layer model, but for our purposes here a four-layer model is most useful, shown in Table 4.1.

The physical layer is the lowest layer, and defines how bits (1s and 0s) are passed between network nodes, normally as electromagnetic or optical signals. The physical layer also handles errors in communications, defines the rules for sharing the network (e.g. what happens if two nodes try to talk at the same time), and has a primitive notion of addresses so that two local nodes can find each other. When a physical layer is in place, the higher layers can assume that there is a capability of sending a piece of binary information reliably from one node to another. Technologies that exist in this layer include ISDN (Integrated Services Digital Network – a special purpose line offering up to 128 kbps speeds), ADSL (Asynchronous Digital Subscriber Line – a technology that uses conventional telephone cabling, but typically achieves about 1.5 mbps downstream speed), Ethernet (the most common local area networking standard), and the hubs and switches that propagate signals around the local network.

The next layer up deals with packets and addresses. This layer introduces the notion of routing, such that every node on an extended network has a unique address, like a street address or telephone number in the real world, and a packet of information, sent from anywhere on the network, will be routed to its destination node. Technologies that work in this space include TCP/IP (Transmission Control Protocol/Internet Protocol – used to address and send packets and manage errors), DNS (Domain Name Service – used to translate between Website names and numeric IP addresses), DHCP (Dynamic Host Configuration Protocol – used to assign IP addresses to client computers), and NAT (Network Address Translation – used to translate between intranet and Internet addresses).

At this layer, the vast majority of networks, and the Internet itself, use Internet Protocol, IP. An extension of IP, called IPv6, is being rolled out gradually. This increases the size of IP addresses from 4 bytes to 16 bytes (creating many more addresses – easily enough for every computer, appliance, human, building, vehicle, and animal on earth), has better support for multimedia streaming, and has support for security in the form of IPSec.

The layer above this is the session layer. Given that the two layers below allow packets of a fixed size (e.g. 2 kilobytes) to be sent reliably between computers anywhere on the network, the session layer uses them to manage an interaction over multiple packets, such as the downloading of a Web page or the transmission of an e-mail message. So, when, for example, a user asks for the website www.amazon.com in her Web browser, the session layer will initiate a session with Amazon's server, ask for all the packets to be sent, reassemble them, then pass them up to the application (in this case the Web browser) to use as it will. Typically, it makes sense to think of the security aspects of a communication occurring at this level also. So, an application making use of this layer can assume it has the ability to have an arbitrarily large/long communication securely with any other node on the network. Session layer technologies include HTTP (HyperText Transfer Protocol – mostly used for transporting Web pages), HTTPS (a secure version of HTTP), FTP (File Transfer Protocol), and SMTP (Simple Mail Transfer Protocol).

The final layer is the networked application layer. This refers to applications, such as Web browsers and e-mail servers, that make use of the network. Note that nowadays almost every application program, from games to enterprise resource planning tools, have some networking component. But, as explained earlier, because of the layered nature of communications, most of these applications will work over any lower layer network protocol. Therefore SAP will run over a fast Ethernet network, or a high-speed fibre optic network.

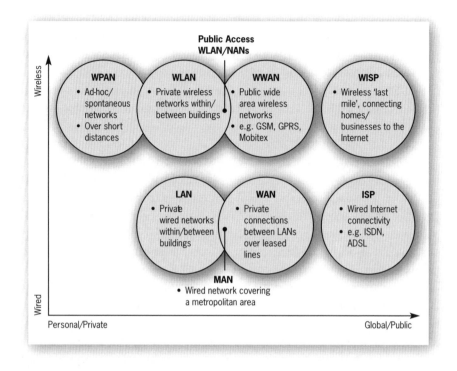

Figure 4.2 A topology of networking.

Types of network

The scope of computer networks is a key determinant of their nature, and hence the technologies that they use. In general, as networks become larger, the bandwidth tends to become costlier, the quality of the link tends to be less reliable, and the need for security increases.

There are typically five classifications of network scope: personal, local area, neighbourhood/metropolitan, wide area, and public/Internet /ISP, as shown in Figure 4.2.

Personal area networks (PANs) are a relatively new concept. These are the networks around an individual, and are typically wireless (WPANs). They connect devices such as a PDA, headset, mobile phone, and MP3 player. It is envisaged that these networks will become more common in future, possibly including various categories of wearable computing and later invasive[8] medical technologies. Bluetooth, discussed

---

[8] Invasive devices are embedded within the human body.

later in this book, is the leading technology in this nascent field. In Bluetooth terms a PAN may sometimes be called a Piconet, with multiple interacting Piconets (several people) called a Scatternet.

Local area networks are the next concept. The LAN is, in general, a network connecting a limited number of devices (typically tens or hundreds, not thousands) within a limited space, such as an office building. As such, LANs tend to be reliable, fairly fast (e.g. 100 Mbits/second), and do not need quite as high a security level as public networks. The most common LAN standard is Ethernet. More recently, two technologies have introduced wireless versions of LANs (WLANs) – WiFi (also known as IEEE802.11b) and Bluetooth. These are discussed more extensively in Chapter 8.

WANs, or wide area networks, are groups of private LANs linked together. A typical WAN would be a large corporation having each of its international offices wired up with LANs, then those LANs linked together with routers and wide area connections and protocols to form their global WAN. In general, WAN links may be either fixed bandwidth leased from telecom providers, like British Telecom, or secure tunnels through the Internet, called VPNs (Virtual Private Networks). VPNs are discussed in more detail in the Security section. Note that the term WWAN, or wireless WAN, is sometimes used to mean the connection of a wireless device, such as a PDA, to the Internet through a cellular network – this is not a wireless version of WAN, and hence is a little confusing.

The largest, and most public, form of network is the Internet, connected to through some form of ISP (Internet Service Provider). More recently, Wireless ISPs have appeared, with the 'last mile' of connection between an office or home and the ISP being achieved with broadband wireless connectivity. Clearly, this is potentially a huge cost saver, massively reducing the unit cost of hooking up a home or office building.

Finally, there are forms of networking appearing called neighbourhood area networks (NANs) and metropolitan area networks (MANs). These are types of networks that are not restricted to one organization (like LANs), but are shared among a group of people within one geographic area for cost reasons. Names are not standardized here, but typically MANs are wired solutions, using MDUs (Multiple Dwelling Units) to allow several homes and/or companies to share one big connection to the Internet. NANs are wireless solutions, using technologies like WiFi to allow multiple wireless users, e.g. in an airport business lounge, to access the Internet from their laptops/PDAs. NANs are described further in Chapter 8.

The following two text boxes discuss MobileStar, a public access WLAN player, and the Starbucks implementation of public access WLAN.

A further distinction among networks is between intra-, extra-, and Internet. Typically, an intranet runs inside an organization, often over a LAN, but sometimes over a WAN, allowing trusted members of that organization to access restricted services and information. Intranets normally use Web-like technologies, such as Web browsers.

Extranets are used to allow individuals or companies outside the organization to access the intranet, either using a secure privately leased line, or using Virtual Private Network (VPN) technologies over the Internet. VPNs are discussed in Chapter 5, in the Security section.

The Internet, as everyone knows, is the large public network of networks that allows most computers in the world to connect to each other.

 Key industry player: MobileStar

Founded in Texas in 1997, MobileStar were one of the earliest players to attempt to turn IEEE802.11 wireless LAN technology into a public access WLAN business. MobileStar raised over US$50 million in two rounds of funding to create wireless access points in several hundred hotels, airport lounges, and coffee shops.

Location partners included Hilton hotels, Starbucks coffee shops, and American Airlines Admirals' Club lounges. Technology partners included Proxim and Cisco.

Despite being one of the first public access WLANs to achieve critical mass, a great deal of positive feedback from customers, and a substantial deal with Starbucks, MobileStar recently ran out of money, and have been bought by Voicestream Wireless, itself acquired shortly afterwards by T-Mobile (the wireless arm of Deutsche Telekom). Nevertheless, analysts believe that the public access WLAN business shows promise, perhaps not as a pure play competitor to 3G data services, but as a complement to them.

Real world example: Starbucks WLAN service

In 2000, Starbucks announced that they would offer a wireless LAN service in 4000 of their coffee shops by the end of 2002. At the end of 2001, 600 stores had been 'unwired up'.

This service allow Starbucks customers to access the Internet while drinking their cappuccino, either using their own laptop or PDA with a WLAN card inserted, or by borrowing a Compaq WLAN-enabled PDA from the shop.

The service partner is MobileStar, who already have several hundred WLAN Internet access points in the United States, in airports and hotel public areas. Participating customers are required to be MobileStar members, paying a monthly fee for access. Other partners in this venture were Compaq (wireless terminals) and Microsoft (ISP).

The initiative was in a lull after MobileStar's purchase by Voicestream Wireless, until August 2002 when T-Mobile, the new owner, announced jointly with Starbucks and Hewlett Packard a plan to expand the network from the current levels of 1200 stores to 2000 stores by end 2002, including some non-US sites.

This is an interesting, highly public, spearhead into the envisaged world of neighbourhood area networks.

The anatomy of the Internet

Next, we will draw a simplified picture of the Internet, showing all the pieces enabling businesses and individuals to connect to Web-based services. Before putting them together, we will review each of the pieces.

Starting from the top left in Figure 4.3, the first piece is a client computer. Typically, this is a PC, but client computers may also be Macintoshes, Unix/Linux workstations, or PDAs.

Next comes the server. A server is often almost identical to a client computer, but with more emphasis on processing and storage power, and less on human input/output technologies, like graphics and sound cards. Also, as we will see later, servers run special applications such as Web servers and e-commerce servers.

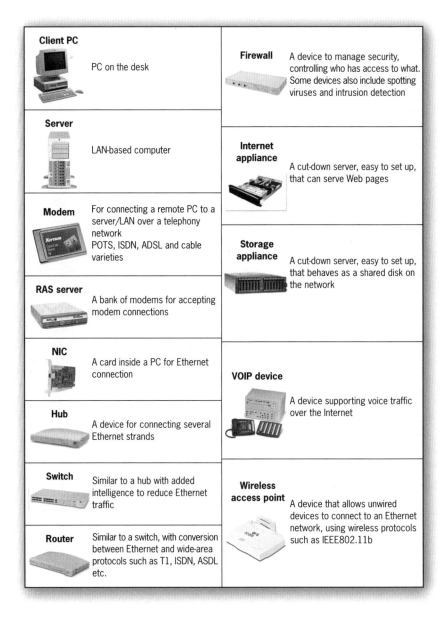

Client PC		Firewall	A device to manage security, controlling who has access to what. Some devices also include spotting viruses and intrusion detection
	PC on the desk		
Server	LAN-based computer	**Internet appliance**	A cut-down server, easy to set up, that can serve Web pages
Modem	For connecting a remote PC to a server/LAN over a telephony network POTS, ISDN, ADSL and cable varieties	**Storage appliance**	A cut-down server, easy to set up, that behaves as a shared disk on the network
RAS server	A bank of modems for accepting modem connections		
NIC	A card inside a PC for Ethernet connection	**VOIP device**	A device supporting voice traffic over the Internet
Hub	A device for connecting several Ethernet strands		
Switch	Similar to a hub with added intelligence to reduce Ethernet traffic	**Wireless access point**	A device that allows unwired devices to connect to an Ethernet network, using wireless protocols such as IEEE802.11b
Router	Similar to a switch, with conversion between Ethernet and wide-area protocols such as T1, ISDN, ASDL etc.		

Figure 4.3 The pieces of the Internet.

The modem is the device which allows computers to connect over wide area links, such as normal telephone lines, ISDN and ADSL connections, and cable connections. Modems translate the digital signals into formats that can be interpreted across telecoms networks. Increasingly modems are not physically visible, but are embedded inside desktop and laptop computers.

A RAS server[9] (Remote Access Server) is essentially a bank of modems, typically deployed at an ISP's facilities or in a corporate data centre, ready to receive data calls from remote users through their modems.

A Network Interface Card (NIC) is the interface between a computer and a LAN, e.g. an Ethernet LAN. As with modems, NICs are increasingly built into computers.

Hubs, switches, and routers form the plumbing of the networks of the Internet. Hubs are dumb boxes, simply allowing all the nodes on the LAN to talk to each other. Typically, a very small company (fewer than 10 users) might plug all its PCs into a hub. A hub propagates every packet sent in to it to every other line connected to it. A switch is like a hub with additional intelligence, filtering traffic such that packets not destined for nodes on a particular connection are not propagated down that line. This improves performance as the volume of traffic increases.

A router is used to convert between wide area protocols (such as ISDN) and the corporate LAN, allowing a corporate LAN to connect to an ISP, or to the corporate WAN. For small companies, there are all-in-one boxes that perform as switches and routers (and often as firewalls as well).

The largest manufacturers of hubs, switches, and routers is Cisco. Others include 3Com, Bay Networks (owned by Lucent), and a number of Taiwanese low-cost players such as Linksys and D-Link.

A firewall is a device that controls access to and from the LAN. Typically, a firewall splits the network into three parts – the intranet, the Internet, and a DMZ (demilitarized zone). The Internet is a completely public, untrusted zone, where all incoming packets must be viewed with suspicion. An intranet is a completely private, trusted zone, where only

---

[9] Astute readers will note that the word server is redundant here, as the S of RAS stands for server. This issue is common in computing (cf. DNS server, RAID disks), and, since this book is about understanding and communicating with technology and technologists, we have chosen to follow convention.

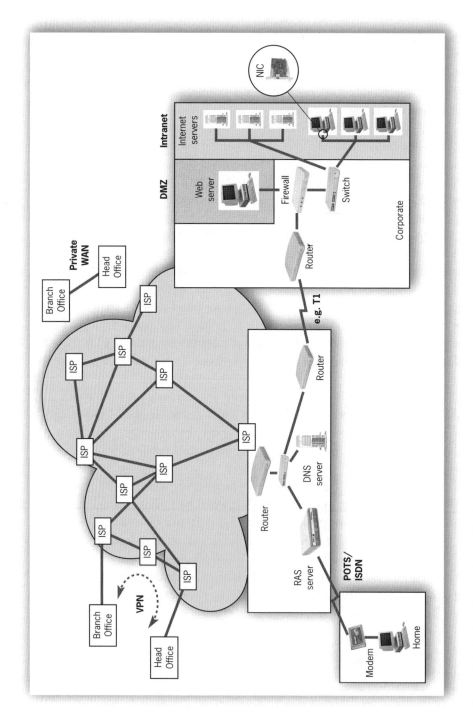

Figure 4.4 A simplified picture of the Internet.

corporate users should have access. The DMZ is typically where the corporate Web presence is kept – with untrusted users given limited access (enabling them to interact with the company's Web presence).

More sophisticated firewalls also include intrusion detection logic, looking for known hacking behaviours and scanning for viruses. Note that firewalls/intrusion detection devices may be either physical boxes or software running on a general purpose server.

Most of the network plumbing manufacturers mentioned above have an OEM firewall offering, with firewall-specific brands including Checkpoint and Sonic. (Note that OEM stands for Original Equipment Manufacturer, and refers to a business model where a brand owner, e.g. Cisco, brands a product manufactured by another company, e.g. Checkpoint.)

Other devices that may appear on the Internet include Internet appliances and Voice over IP (VOIP) devices. Internet appliances are trimmed-down servers designed to perform one specific task more quickly, cheaply, and reliably than a general purpose server, e.g. serving Web pages (Web appliances) or serving storage (Storage appliances). Internet appliances are also called thinservers. There are many startups in this area, but probably the best established player is Network Appliance.

VOIP devices allow voice calls to be made over an IP (Internet Protocol) data network. Devices needed to achieve this include IP handsets and IP PBXs (Private Branch Exchanges). VOIP penetration is still limited, mainly due to the Quality of Service (QoS) problem mentioned earlier.

Figure 4.4 shows a simplified picture of the Internet, using the components explained above.

The one piece we have not covered yet is the DNS server (Domain Name Server). The DNS server is a general purpose server, running a DNS server application, which is responsible for converting Web addresses (e.g. www.ebay.com) into IP addresses (e.g. 128.136.0.1).

Note that, for simplicity, the connections between ISPs are shown as a cloud of unstructured connections. In fact, the ISPs are organized in a hierarchy. Typically, local ISPs connect to regional ISPs, who in turn connect to national and international ISPs. The highest tier, national and international ISPs, connect to each other using Network Access Points (NAPs), which are very complex, high-speed switching centres.

3Com and Citrix are two key players in the data networking industry, described in the following text boxes.

Key industry player: 3Com

3Com are one of the oldest players in the data networking industry. The company was founded by Bob Metcalfe, one of the inventors of Ethernet. Once a giant of the NASDAQ, 3Com's revenues shrank from US$5.2 billion in 1999 to US$4.3 billion in 2000, US$2.8 billion in 2001, and US$1.5 billion in 2002.

3Com's primary products are data networking infrastructure, including hubs, switches, routers, firewalls, modems, and 'voice over IP' boxes.

Through the 1990s, 3Com settled into an IBM-like large company at the top of the tree, but were the subject of a strategic squeeze. Cisco, the darling of many business school cases and investors, embarked on a spree of successful M&A activities, and took the 'high concept' position of the corporate data networking player of choice. Meanwhile a series of low-cost players, such as D-Link and Linksys from Taiwan, took the low-cost position.

3Com were also somewhat derailed by the purchase of US Robotics, a strong modem player, who owned the Palm PDA. Although never a huge percentage of 3Com's revenues, Palm occupied a great deal of share of mind of senior management, and was damaging to strategic focus until its recent spin-off.

Key industry player: Citrix

Citrix are the dominant player in the provision of thin-client infrastructure. Their core technology asset is Metaframe/ICA (Independent Computing Architecture). This technology allows applications to be run on a server, with client computers simply running the ICA client, connecting to that server over the network. In this way an end-user experiences the application (e.g. Microsoft Word) just as if they were running it on their PC, but the application actually executes on a centralized server. There are many benefits to this approach, including massively reduced rollout/upgrade costs, reduced power needs, and hence cost of the client computer, and reduced maintenance needs. Further, this architecture allows Windows™ programs to run on non-Windows platforms, as long as Citrix supports

▶

Key industry player *Continued*

that platform. The only real drawback is increased dependence on the network. Without the network, the client computer becomes useless.

Citrix have built a very strong business, with revenues rising from US$470 million in 2000 to US$592 million in 2001, with net income of US$105 million. They have also maintained deep ties with Microsoft, with Microsoft licensing certain aspects of the Citrix platform in their Terminal Services product from 1997 to 2002, and a deal being signed in 2002 giving Citrix access to the Microsoft Windows™ code.

Further, Citrix represent a strong platform for the Application Service Provider (ASP) business, where a third party hosts all a company's applications, and provides them over a network link. The jury is still out on whether the ASP business will take off, but, if it does, Citrix are well positioned to gain from it.

Management perspectives

Networking (the ability to share information easily with little regard for time or space) has clearly been one of the major advancements in technology in terms of its potential impact on business. The following is a list of issues for managers to consider with regard to networking:

- What are my organization's current policies for sharing information within the company? In other words, if information is power, should everyone have access to most information in order to improve organizational learning or ensure people are working from a common perspective?
- Similarly, what impact does networking have on information flows and the power structure within my company? What does the real organizational chart look like?
- What are my organization's current policies for sharing information outside the company? Does the technology match the policy?
- How robust is my corporate network? Is the spend on robustness/ continuity commensurate with the impact that network downtime would have?

CHAPTER

5

The Web and e-commerce
The transition from information superhighway to transaction superhighway

Concepts covered in this chapter

- How the Web works – requesting a Web page
- The role of advanced Web technologies, including XML and XSL, applets, streaming, security, and payment
- A detailed exposition of the different aspects of computer security, common threats, and tools to secure systems
- A description of Content Distribution Network player Akamai, the court case between media companies Canal Plus and NDS, and a real world hacking problem from xtempus, a mobile Internet startup

Questions to ponder before reading

- What is the difference between the Internet and the World Wide Web?
- What happens behind the scenes when you try to access a Web site using a browser?
- What is the role of the following advanced technologies: Javascript, Java applets, streaming support, ASP, XML, XSL, cookies, Content Distribution Networks?
- Other than preserving confidentiality, what are the aspects of computer security?
- What are the major forms of security threat to e-commerce systems, and what are the main tools to combat them?

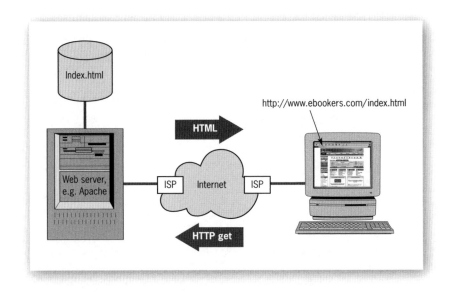

Figure 5.1 Getting a Web page.

Basic Web technologies

The World Wide Web (WWW) sits on top of the Internet, and is the technology that supports Web browsers and Web pages. Although e-mail and file transfer (FTP) are other uses for the Internet, the WWW is by far the most prevalent.

Using Figure 5.1, we will explain how the most basic Web transaction – getting a Web page – happens. Suppose you, as a user, type in http:// www.ebookers.com to your Web browser, e.g. Internet Explorer. The first thing the Web browser does is, using the HTTP session protocol, attempt to establish a session with www.ebookers.com. The lower layers convert www.ebookers.com to an IP address, such as 129.46.0.4, using the Domain Name Service (DNS), then the router within the ISP routes a packet to lastminute's Web server. The Web server will be running a Web server application, the most prevalent of which is Apache. That Web server software validates whether you, as an Internet-based stranger, have permission to open the home page of ebookers. You are then sent back the homepage, which in the simplest case will be a page described in HTML (HyperText Markup Language). The session layer

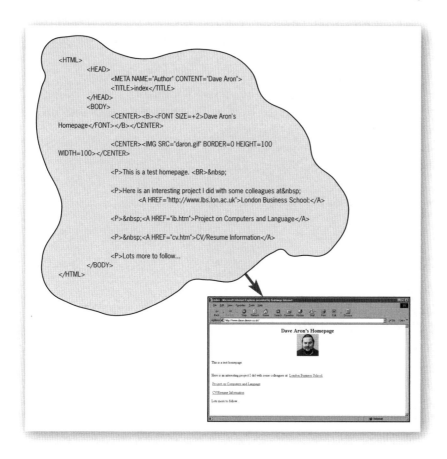

Figure 5.2 How HTML works.

will reassemble the page from all the packets it arrived in, then pass that page back to the Web browser, which knows how to interpret and display HTML pages.

An example of an HTML page and how it looks when displayed in a Web browser is shown in Figure 5.2. Essentially HTML allows you to create a page of text, then add a few special 'markup tags' like <CEN-TER>, <IMG>, or <A>, which are either instructions as to how to format some of the text, instructions to include a picture file, or links to other pages. This page description capability provides the basics needed for a Web experience.

The functionality missing in the above, but still essential for a fully functional Internet, includes:

- support for streaming media, e.g. video;
- support for a richer user experience than HTML can offer (pop-up menus etc.);
- support for multiple client devices, e.g. PDA, WAP phone;
- support for personalization of content within and across sessions;
- interaction with traditional back end software (e.g. ERP systems);
- management of security;
- the ability to receive payment;
- the ability to scale solutions, and remove any single points of failure;
- management of Internet performance.

Advanced Web technologies

The Web, as initially conceived, was a way of sharing documents and linking them with hyperlinks. As the Web has been used by more and more consumers and businesses, it has been stretched in various ways, to turn it into an incredibly powerful multimedia information, entertainment, and transaction medium. Table 5.1 lists the key additional components of the Web, layered on to the basic skeleton described above to achieve this.

Table 5.1 Advanced Web technologies.

Feature	Technologies
Dynamic pages	DHTML, Javascript
Richer (personalized) interface	CSS, XML/XSL
Downloadable applets	Java applets, ActiveX controls
Streaming and multimedia	RealAudio/Video, Flash
Searchability	Search engines
Server interaction	CGI, ASP, JSP/Java, Perl
Sessions and personalization	Cookies
Security	HTTPS, encryption
Payment services	E-commerce servers, payment
Scaling and robustness	Load balancing servers, app servers
Internet performance	CDN

1. Richer, more dynamic page description languages

The great thing about HTML and Web browsers is that they are stand-ard, simple, and ubiquitous. The Web proliferated because of this – as soon as a Web-based service pops up anywhere in the world, it can be accessed by any Internet-connected PC with a Web browser.

The downside of this is that typically a Web-based application is much less user-friendly than a conventional program installed on your computer. A good way to think of this is to compare using a locally resident e-mail client, like Microsoft Outlook or Lotus Notes, with a Web-based e-mail client, such as Yahoo or Hotmail's e-mail offering.

Although HTML has improved slowly over the years, industry players felt that a quantum leap in usability was necessary for the continuing transition to Web-based services. Two technologies help with this: Dynamic HTML (DHTML) and Javascript. Both of these are interpreted languages that sit within Web pages, and allow for much more sophistic-ated interaction, like pop-up menus, and areas that change when the mouse passes over them (hotspots).

The most popular Web browsers, Internet Explorer and Netscape Navigator, both offer support for DHTML and Javascript.

2. Personalized/customized pages

Over and above more friendly user interfaces, there is a need for person-alized Web experiences, that is Web services that are tailored to the cus-tomer's needs, either explicitly (through the user stating preferences), or implicitly (using intelligent learning technologies that we will deal with later in the book). These needs may include personal preferences, the type of device they are using, the location from which they are accessing, and the time of access.

Cascading Style Sheets (CSS) were the first technology to address the formatting aspects of this issue, allowing users to apply a 'style sheet' to a Web page – changing it according to their preferences.

A more comprehensive solution is the use of Extensible Markup Language (XML) and Extensible Style Sheet (XSL) technologies. XML has many uses, but, in the context of personalized Web pages, the archi-tecture of a Web service is changed such that, instead of having a single program that generates Web pages using HTML, DHTML, etc., the pro-gram is split into two layers, such that the main application generates XML (a high-level description of the user interaction required), then a presentation layer program is created that uses style rules, written using

XSL technologies, that allow the XML content to be presented in a format suitable for the end-user, the device and browser they are using.

This allows the same 'back-end' business rules to be applied to multiple user interfaces, reducing the likelihood of bugs or inconsistencies if the presentation code was embedded in the business rules.

The separate presentation layer and 'business rules' layer represent the front two layers of the much touted 'Three Layer Architecture', explained in more detail in Chapter 6.

3. Downloadable applets

For many applications and services, the Web represents an excellent distribution and communication channel, but a page-oriented interface in a Web browser is entirely inappropriate. An example might be a downloadable arcade game. As explained in Chapter 3, for such applications, Java allows applets to be downloaded over the Web to a client computer, and then executed by a Java Virtual Machine (JVM) on that computer, allowing a much more general purpose experience than a Web front end. Microsoft created a similar concept to applets, known as Active X controls. Active X builds on a number of earlier Microsoft technologies (COM – Component Object Model, DCOM – Distributed Component Object Model, OLE – Object Linking and Embedding) to achieve distributable network components.

4. Streaming multimedia and animation

As bandwidth improved, the Web became a more realistic channel for multimedia, including video and audio. The need to stream multimedia, i.e. download and play video/audio, is quite challenging, and cannot use high-level protocols, like HTTP, as it is more 'real time' in nature, downloading a bit at a time. There are a number of applications and protocols, which are 'pluggable' into a Web browser like Internet Explorer, to handle streaming media.

The most successful player in this area so far is Real Networks, with its RealAudio and RealVideo technologies.

5. Searchability

As the Web grows larger, and is used by a wider and wider group of communities for more and more purposes, it has greater and greater potential. However, the reason for its growth is also a reason for its major challenge – lack of structure.

The only requirement of a Web service is that it can present HTML pages over an HTTP transport from a recognized IP address. Other than that pages and services can be structured in any way at all, and hence can be both unique and very dynamic for any service. This has resulted in the interesting situation that, if one wants to know any fact on almost any subject, it is almost certainly on the Web, but it may be incredibly difficult to find it (and also to verify its accuracy). Another symptom of this issue is observing new Web users not knowing 'where to start.'

This challenge has been taken up by the portals, and behind them Web search engines. Some famous search brands of the past few years include Altavista, Yahoo, Hotbot, Excite, Infoseek, Lycos, MetaCrawler, AskJeeves, Alltheweb/FAST, Google, iWon, Northern Light, OpenText, Vivisimo, and LookSmart.

Broadly speaking, the Web search capabilities can be segmented into three categories: search engines, meta-search engines, and Web directories. Search engines (like Google) allow a keyword-based search of the Web, meta-search engines (like LookSmart) combine the results of several search engines, while Web directories (like Yahoo) attempt to organize Web pages and services in an easily navigable tree structure. Some search brands combine all three of these.

Search engines send 'webcrawling' programs off to search the Web, then store keywords from Web pages in their vast databases. Generally search engines are pushing the boundaries of computing capabilities, with multiterabyte databases, massively parallel processing, and high uptime/reliability requirements.

The key success factors (KSFs) for search engines include breadth of coverage and speed of search. The KSF for meta-search engines is primarily clarity of presentation. For directories, clarity of organization and intelligence in topic inferencing are key.

Search engines have tended to differentiate on richness of query logic (i.e. users can ask complex questions), specialized search (e.g. picture, video), natural language input capability, natural translation capability, and the ability to infer topics of user interest automatically and intelligently.

Search engine business models are also complex, ranging from straightforward technology licensing to portal models (advertising, building community, etc.).

6. *Server application interaction*

The picture painted in the previous section referred to Web servers delivering static Web pages. In reality, a great deal of Web activity represents the interaction of Web-based clients with live applications through the Web. Examples include remote access to e-mail services (e.g. Lotus Notes, Microsoft Exchange), and Web terminal access to ERP applications such as SAP or Peoplesoft.

This requires an extra piece of the puzzle, the ability for an HTTP request to trigger not just the retrieval of a Web page, but the invocation of any computer program, e.g. a program to calculate an employee's national insurance contribution. CGI, or Common Gateway Interface, was the first approach here, allowing interpreted scripts in languages such as Perl to be invoked by HTTP requests.

Two other major technologies here are ASP and JSP, Active Server Pages and Java Server Pages. These represent standard ways to get Web servers such as Apache, originally designed just to serve Web pages, to invoke programs and database functions, and capture the results to a Web page. ASP is the technology that is designed to work within a Microsoft environment, whereas JSP is the equivalent for a Java environment.

There are also more proprietary approaches taken by some Web server companies, probably the most widespread being Macromedia's Cold Fusion, a very rich Web environment with its own method of scripting.

7. *Session personalization*

As discussed in the last chapter, HTTP manages online requests for Web pages, establishing an electronic session that will last for the lifetime of many TCP packets, and ensure that a complete page is captured and displayed during the session.

Similarly, there is a need for a relationship to exist between a Web user and a Web service provider, which lasts across many electronic sessions, such that personalized settings and general knowledge of the user can last for the lifetime of the relationship. A key technology for achieving this is cookies. A cookie is deposited on the user's computer, containing information allowing the Web service to identify that user and their history and preferences. An alternative to cookies is simply a Web login process, where a user is asked to supply a username and password, then all session and personalization information is stored on the server, and associated with that username.

8. Security

As the Web becomes increasingly a transactional, rather than just an informational, channel, security becomes imperative for widespread acceptance. Security is a huge topic, and the next section deals with it in detail.

9. Payment

In order to provide a transactional Web, a method of payment is necessary. There are various requirements and areas of focus, including payment for Web shopping and services, person-to-person (P2P) payments, micropayments, and wireless payments. There are also some loyalty-point-like services, which are not full payment systems, but can be used for purchasing from participating services.

A plethora of online payment offerings have sprung up in the last few years, including Beenz, Billpoint, Cyberbucks, Cybercash, Digicash, eCash, Flooz, Paybox, PayDirect, Paypal, and Worldpay. Some have flourished, some have died, and some have been acquired by more general companies, such as eBay. Also, the real world payment brands, such as American Express, Mastercard, and Visa, have taken more significant stakes in online payment mechanisms.

10. Scaling and robustness

For reliable Web services, it is essential that uptime is high, i.e. that services do not break down too often. As discussed in Chapter 3, many Web developers talk about five nines, or 99.999% availability, for the Web to begin to feel as reliable as the fixed telephone network.

Designing systems that are highly reliable, also called robust systems, revolves around the concept of redundancy. Normally a negative term, in computing redundant systems are systems where there is more than one of each component, and the architecture of the system is such that, if any one component fails, another picks up its duties, ideally transparently to the user. Hence a reliable system is redundant, with no single points of failure.

A closely related challenge is scalability, creating systems that can run across many boxes, so that, when higher volumes are called for, the number of boxes can simply be increased. Hence, robust, scalable Web services will be designed to run across multiple boxes, each remaining in synchronization with the others, with no single points of failure.

> **Key industry player:** Akamai
>
> Founded in 1998 out of MIT (Massachusetts Institute of Technology), Akamai were the first player to create a content distribution network (CDN) business. By using intelligent routing algorithms, Akamai allow their clients to place high-bandwidth content on the Akamai CDN, resulting in a better Web experience for their clients' customers.
>
> Based on the CDN concept, Akamai have expanded their business quickly, including streaming media services and business intelligence. Revenues were US$4 million in 1999, rising to US$90 million in 2000 and US$163 million in 2001.

11. Internet performance tuning

Another deficiency of the basic Internet architecture is the ability to ensure that content downloads fast. Because Internet content is routed dynamically through many routers, which are not owned by either the service provider or the end-user, it is impossible to guarantee the quality of the user experience.

A category of company called content distribution network (CDN) has appeared to help with this challenge. CDNs allow their clients' high-bandwidth and streaming content (video, audio, pictures) to be stored in their network. Many copies of that content will then be kept on their 'edge servers', scattered around the Internet. Then, when customers of their clients request some high-bandwidth content, they will be redirected to the CDN's server closest to them, resulting in much improved customer experience.

The founder of and leader in this field is Akamai (see text box above), but it has since become a lucrative sub-industry. There are currently efforts in progress to standardize this concept, called 'Edge Side Includes' (ESI).

Computer security

What is computer security?

Security has always been an issue in computing, primarily because the key assets are informational, and not physical, hence data is more open to covert theft, and communications are more open to being intercepted

Table 5.2 Aspects of computer security.

Concept	Ideal
Privacy	Unauthorized parties cannot track what you are doing, or who you are talking to
Confidentiality	Messages cannot be overheard by others
Integrity	Messages can be guaranteed complete and not tampered with
Authentication	Identity of sender and/or receiver can be guaranteed
Non-repudiation	Neither party can deny that a transaction took place
Availability	Unauthorized parties cannot disrupt or deny service

secretly – since data can be replicated very simply while leaving the original intact.

Security is important for any system, but becomes increasingly important as the Web spreads in scope (geographically and across areas of our life), and is used more and more for value-based transactions.

As an indicator of the size of the issue, research company Computer Economics estimated that the damage from viruses, worms, and trojan horses (defined below) totalled US$13.2 billion in 2001. (The good news is that this was down from US$17.1 billion in 2000.) Looking at the e-commerce area, Internet payment fraud totalled $1.6 billion worldwide in 2000.[10]

Computer security can be thought of as having six aspects, shown in Table 5.2.

A computer security policy must have components that address each of the aspects listed in the table, combined with a physical security policy.

How they hack

Computer hacking is a complex discipline, and constantly changing. Table 5.3 lists the common forms of attack that hackers would use to try to compromise security, motivated commercially (e.g. industrial espionage), ethically/morally, or more likely just for the fun or challenge.

---

[10] Source: Meridien Research.

Table 5.3 Common forms of security threat.

IP/DNS spoofing	Performing a transaction while pretending to be someone else
Viruses/trojan horses/ logic bombs/worms	Inserting a piece of code that damages, or simply floods, a computer, then replicates itself
Denial of service	Flooding a server with packets to prevent genuine users from accessing services
Sniffing	Listening to all packets on a network
Replay attack	Capturing, then replaying, genuine transactions
Man-in-the-middle	Sitting between two parties, replicating the conversation between them, capturing all packets

1. IP/DNS spoofing

IP (Internet Protocol) addresses are the four-part addresses[11] that are the unique identifiers of the Internet. DNS (Domain Name Service) is the function that allows services to be defined by names (e.g. www.amazon.com), which are then translated to IP addresses (e.g. 100.123.42.4). IP/DNS spoofing refers to hackers masquerading as a legitimate IP address/DNS name in order to gain unauthorized access.

2. Viruses/trojan horses/logic bombs/worms

This class of attack involves inserting a piece of damaging code into a system. For clarity, viruses are code that damage the host system and replicate themselves, trojan horses are viruses hidden inside legitimate programs, logic bombs are viruses which lie dormant, triggered by specific logical conditions, e.g. the system date reaching a specific date, like Da Vinci's birthday. Finally, worms replicate, but do no damage to the system. Worms damage a network's functionality by flooding the communications bandwidth with their replication needs. Note that all of the types of attack, like real biological viruses, are difficult to stop, as they have no 'master' computer or process, but are genuinely distributed. A further difficulty is viruses that mutate over time, making simple pattern matching techniques ineffective in catching them.

---

[11] Note that IPV6, a new version of IP being rolled out gradually, extends this addressing mechanism significantly, preparing for the 'era of ubiquitous computing', where every computer, vehicle, appliance, person, and possibly even animal has an IP address!

3. Denial of service

This refers to an attack which, like vandalism, is focused not on gaining unauthorized access, but damaging/occupying a system such that authorized users lose access, as the system is so busy fighting off attacks.

4. Sniffing

This refers to illegally listening to every packet of information on a network (whoever it is intended for), then taking the information away to decrypt/use later. Vulnerability to sniffing is an inevitable downside of a packet-based network, where most information is passed to many network nodes. Sniffing normally requires physical access to a network. With the advent of wireless networking, sniffing becomes particularly scary, as it may be possible from outside the building, or even from a passing vehicle (dubbed 'drive-by hacking' by the press; see the section on mobile security).

5. Replay attack

Even if hackers are unable to decrypt a transaction, they may be able to capture packets, work out who they were sent from and to, then resend them one or more times. Similar to denial of service, this is more of a vandal's approach than an approach useful for gaining information.

6. Man in the middle

A man in the middle attack occurs where a hacker manages to get their computer between two legitimate parties, and replicates all packets going both ways, while capturing them for later analysis. This approach facilitates both sniffing and replay attacks.

Security enforcement

The tools available to the security manager include the following (see also Table 5.4).

1. Authentication mechanisms

These technologies allow the user to identify who they are. There are four classes of mechanism currently available. Passwords and challenges represent the user typing in a secret code to identify him- or herself. (Challenges are slightly more sophisticated than passwords, generally asking a question from a predetermined set, e.g. what is your mother's

Table 5.4 Tools for security management.

Authentication Mechanisms	Passwords/challenges, tokens/smartcards, digital certificates (X509), biometrics
Encryption	Encoding messages, so that they are unreadable without a key. Symmetric or assymetric (PKI) approaches
Firewalls	Network devices that partition the network logically and control who and what can access which segments (Intranet, DMZ, Internet). May be hardware or software
Intrusion Detection Devices	Network devices that look for known hacking behaviours and or viruses. May be co-located with firewall
Proxy Servers	Server that pretends to be a server on your network, but allows arbitrarily complex packet inspection before release
Security Consultants	Security audits and/or ethical hacking

maiden name?) Tokens and smartcards are physical objects that the user must possess, e.g. 'dongles' that plug into the back of a computer, or smartcards that are swiped through a card reader. Digital certificates are the online equivalent of a signature held by a certification authority (CA) online. One example of a CA is the company Verisign. Finally, biometrics refers to techniques that use some aspect of the user's physical person to identify that person. Currently available biometric technologies include fingerprints, handprints, voice authentication, iris recognition, and face recognition. Needless to say, as many of the above techniques as desired can be used together to further thwart an attacker.

2. Encryption

Encryption refers to techniques used to render a message meaningless if intercepted by an unauthorized party. Encryption has a much longer history than computing, and was used in ancient wars, e.g. by the Romans.[12] Conventionally, encryption required a shared secret, or password, known only to sender and receiver, agreed between them in some secure place. This presented a problem in the e-commerce world, as there is no way for, e.g. a consumer in China, to buy a report from a

---

[12] This topic is well covered in Simon Singh's 'The Code Book'.

US company online, with a shared secret. Hence an innovative technique, called Public Key Infrastructure (PKI), was invented. This is described in the next section.

3. Firewalls

Firewalls are a method of keeping unwanted users out of a network, restricting access for some users coming in, and also restricting access out from inside. As discussed in Chapter 4, networks are typically split into three broad zones: intranets, the DMZ, and the Internet. Users going from one of these zones to another are treated differently from each other. Further, most firewalls are able to do more granular controls, e.g. specific users (IP addresses) can be limited to accessing specific services. Note that a firewall can be a separate, special purpose box, or it can be software run on a general purpose computer. Typically, the separate box approach is viewed as more secure, as it makes the firewall itself less vulnerable to attack. All the major networking vendors, such as Cisco, Lucent (through Bay), and 3Com have firewall offerings, typically OEM from specialist firewall makers such as Checkpoint, or Sonic.

4. Intrusion detection

Intrusion detection functions are often used to complement firewalls, looking for specific known hacking behaviours, and automatically locking users out when they are identified. As with firewalls, this functionality can be achieved in a specialized piece of hardware, or as software on a general purpose computer.

5. Proxy servers

Using a proxy server means that all transactions with a particular service (e.g. www.ibm.com) go through a first server, pretending to be that service. This first server is a computer, stripped down to ensure it has no security holes, which accepts requests, screens them, then passes them on if appropriate. Because proxy servers are general purpose computers, they can run arbitrarily complex software to check incoming and outgoing requests, including sophisticated firewall and intrusion detection software. Note that, as well as performing security functions, proxy servers can help with performance, through caching and load balancing (described elsewhere in the book). Also note that proxy servers can be an effective solution to denial-of-service attacks, as bogus packets are kept clear of the real servers.

6. Security consultants

Finally, one can use security consultants to perform security audits on the system, noting any issues found, and recommending and/or implementing solutions. There are many tools available to help with audits, a notable one being SATAN, a notorious tool that allows a hacker (or security consultant) to check quickly if known security weaknesses have been plugged or not. More recently, consultants have adopted an ethical hacking approach, where security consultants (often ex-hackers) try to hack the clients' system, within pre-agreed limits, and report the results.

Security technology standards

There are a plethora of technologies used to create secure Internet transactions. Some of the most common ones are explained briefly in Table 5.5.

1. ISO17799/BS17799

Previously a British Standards Institute (BSI) Standard, now becoming an International Standards Organization (ISO) standard, ISO17799 is intended to be a comprehensive approach to security for an organization, and includes ten components:

1. Security policy
2. Security organization (meaning the team responsible for security)
3. Asset classification and control
4. Personnel security
5. Physical and environmental security
6. Communications and operations security
7. Access control
8. Systems development and maintenance
9. Business continuity management
10. Audit and compliance.

2. PKI

PKI, or Public Key Infrastructure, is a method which allows the encrypting of information without prior exchange of secret information (i.e. a password). In a way, it seems nonsensical that such a thing is possible. It uses a technique such that everybody knows how to write (i.e. encode)

Table 5.5   Internet security technologies.

ISO17799/BS7799	Comprehensive International Standards Organization (ISO) standard for organizational security. Previously British Standards Institute standard (BS)
PKI	Public Key Infrastructure. Method of allowing everyone to write, only one to read. Most common is RSA (named after its three inventors)
HTTPS	A secure form of HTTP for e-commerce, with a secure sockets layer (SSL) underneath, providing public key encryption of messages (newer version of SSL called TLS)
PGP	Pretty Good Privacy – a flexible PKI solution, using RSA assymetric and IDEA symmetric
IPSec	IP Security – a comprehensive, low-level security standard, increasing in usage
Radius	Remote Authentication Dial-In User Service – a standard for centralized password management
DES/3DES	Data Encryption Standard – a symmetric eneryption mechanism, used by US. 3DES uses DES 3 times sequentially for increased security
SET	Secure Electronic Trading – Visa/MC/Microsoft/Netscape-developed specific technology for safeguarding credit/debit card transactions (Secure Electronic Trading)
VPNs	Virtual Private Networks (WAN over the Internet). Standards include PPTP, IPSec, L2TP
X509 Digital certificates/Signatures	Method of authentication, using Certification Authorities (e.g. Entrust, Verisign), and digital signatures (reverse PKI)

a message, but no-one knows how to read (i.e. decode) one. This is done using non-reversible functions, called modulo, or remainder. The PKI infrastructure generates a matching pair of encode and decode functions, using very large prime numbers and the remainder function. The encode (or public) key is shared with the world; the decode (or private) key is kept only by the receiver.

At present, it is too computationally intensive to hack PKI where the key size is large, so it is the safest mechanism for e-commerce confidentiality, and is now commonly used. PKI is, however, a little computationally intensive to use, hence in general it is used at the start of a session to share unique passwords, which are then used for the duration of the session.

PKI is also known as asymmetric encryption, whereas password-based encryption may be called symmetric.

3. HTTPS

Earlier we discussed HTTP, as the session layer protocol that manages a Web session. HTTPS is a secure version of HTTP, embedding a 'Secure Sockets Layer' (SSL). SSL includes PKI encryption. Note that a newer version of SSL is called TLS (Transport Layer Security). For HTTPS to work, clearly the computers at both ends must support it.

4. PGP

PGP, or Pretty Good Privacy, is a public domain encryption utility that can be used within e-mail clients, such as MS Outlook or Lotus Notes, or embedded in a custom program.

5. IPSec

IPSec is a comprehensive, low-level, security standard increasingly being embedded in Internet products.

6. Radius

Radius is a standard for centralized management of users' passwords, in fairly common use.

7. DES/3DES

DES is a symmetric standard that was used for many years in US military applications, and thus the export of hardware or software containing DES algorithms was limited. 3DES, or triple DES, refers to the application of three DES transformations, in order to make a message more confidential. In general, DES is currently regarded by the hacking community as a little weak.

8. SET

Secure Electronic Trading, or SET, is a standard for secure credit card transactions, developed by a consortium of Visa, Mastercard, Microsoft, and Netscape, using digital certificates. SET is a fairly 'heavy' standard in terms of processing requirements, and has received some resistance in the industry.

9. *VPNs*

As discussed earlier in the book, Virtual Private Networks are used to tunnel securely across the Internet, to facilitate private WAN connection through the Internet, or remote LAN access for an individual user. Standards for VPN include PPTP and L2TP. IPSEC also contains a VPN standard.

10. *Digital certificates*

Digital certificates are a form of authentication technique, which are more or less the online equivalent of a signature. After creating a digital certificate, you store it with a certification authority (CA). Companies such as Entrust and Verisign are CAs. Counterparties in online transactions can then confirm your identity.

Interestingly, digital certificates use PKI technology in reverse. In PKI encryption, everyone knows how to write a message to you, but only you know how to read it. For digital certificates, only you know how to write your signature, but everyone can read it.

X.509 is the predominant standard for digital certificates.

At the time of writing there are two interesting initiatives regarding computer security. The first is the TCPA, or Trusted Computing Platform Alliance, founded by Intel, Microsoft, IBM, Compaq, and Hewlett-Packard. In simple terms, TCPA aims to create a secure, 'uncorruptible' core within a PC that cannot be hacked, and makes sure that every other part of the system, both hardware and software, is in some sense approved. The goals of this alliance are credible solutions to software piracy and digital rights management issues, as well as virus protection and more general security enhancements. The second initiative, announced in June 2002, is Microsoft's Palladium. Details are still unclear, but it seems that Palladium represents an effort to build all of the goals of TCPA and more into future versions of Microsoft's Windows™ operating systems.

To complete the security section, the following two text boxes are examples of security issues in the real world.

Real world example: Canal Plus versus NDS

At the time of writing of this book, Canal Plus have just sued NDS for losses of US$1 billion. Both are pay TV companies, the latter a part of Rupert Murdoch's News Corp.

Pay TV involves the use of encrypted cards, which govern which channels a user is entitled to watch. Clearly, it is essential for the encryption mechanism to remain confidential, so that illegal access to pay channels is unachievable.

Canal Plus allege that NDS spent around US$5 million, and employed a good deal of specialized equipment, to crack the Canal Plus encryption technology, then publish an explanation on hacking Web site DR7.com anonymously.

Independent hackers claim that pay TV encryption is crackable without the use of complex equipment.

Since the case began, Vivendi has put Canal Plus up for sale. Ironically, NDS showed interest in acquiring it, but in the end it was sold to Thomson Multimedia. More recently, a number of others have sued NDS, including Measat and DirecTV. The cases are ongoing at the time of writing, although some dealings between Vivendi and News Corp. may include the dropping of the case.

Management perspectives

The Internet and e-commerce have been among the most talked about technologies of recent times. Having gone through the days of hope and hype, here are some key managerial issues:

- Is my firm – facilitated by the Internet – taking advantage of potential new customers and suppliers, who may be located over a much larger geographical area? This can often have huge potential cost savings, as we have seen the rise of distributed manufacturing taking off in Asia, and the rise of remote call centres in countries such as India.

Real world example: xtempus security breach

xtempus is a mobile Internet startup, founded at the end of 1999. In 2000 and early 2001, Dave Aron (co-author) was the CTO of xtempus, running a small team of developers. From the beginning, we had a good small team of system administrators, but in late 2000 we employed a contract security manager to perform security audits and develop security procedures for us. At the time, we felt that this was the right thing to do (just like buying insurance), rather than believing there would be real threats.

Soon into our security manager's time with us, he found a small program that had been placed on our systems. This program took copies of some key data files, and moved them out to a server on the Internet.

Our security manager removed the program, and tried to ensure that no such breach would be possible again, but was unable to trace how the program arrived, or who owned or was accessing the Internet-based target for the file transfer.

After much analysis and contemplation, two important lessons emerged from this incident for us. One was that, with a great deal of staff turnover (use of many short-term contractors), threats are likely to come from within as well as without. The other lesson was that security can never be perfect, and it is all a matter of costs. The key is to increase the cost of hacking in to the point that the effort outweighs the attractiveness.

- How does this access to greater numbers of suppliers, customers, and potential competitors change the balance of power within my industry?
- What are competitors, suppliers, and customers doing with regard to changing business models and the use of Internet-based technologies?
- Is my organization adequately protected against the potential security threats that these new globally connected technologies represent?
- Does my organization have, or should it have, coordinated intranet, Internet, and extranet policies?
- In the next 2–3 years, what changes are likely to occur in Internet and e-commerce technologies? What additional opportunities and/or threats will these represent to my business?

CHAPTER

6

The mobile/multimodal Internet

Concepts covered in this chapter

- The difference between mobile Internet and fixed Internet
- A discussion of why the Japanese i-Mode offering has been so successful
- The layers of the mobile Internet
- All the different standards related to the mobile Internet, including GSM, CDMA, GPRS, 3G, WAP, J2ME
- Implications of faster mobile speeds for IT applications
- New messaging formats, such as MMS
- The use of three-layer architectures in the multimodal Internet context
- Mobile security considerations, including a 'drive-by hacking' example

Questions to ponder before reading

- What is exciting about mobile Internet?
- Why is the mobile Internet different from the fixed Internet?
- What exactly is third-generation (3G) mobile telephony?
- What will all the fancy new phones and networks do for companies and individuals?
- How does security change in a mobile/wireless world?
- What does multimodal Internet mean?

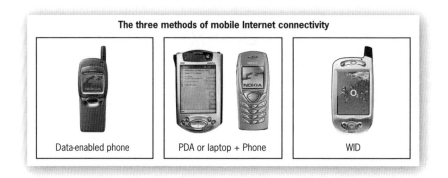

Figure 6.1 The three methods of mobile Internet connectivity. (Sources: Nokia, Compaq, O_2)

What is different about the mobile Internet?

The mobile Internet refers to users accessing the Web from devices while they are mobile, typically mobile phones with WAP or i-Mode functionality, personal digital assistants (PDAs) such as Palm Pilots or laptops connected to the Internet through a mobile phone, or wireless information devices (WIDs), which are an emerging class of device combining the function of a PDA with a phone. See Figure 6.1.

Note that typically the term mobile Internet would not include the use of laptops accessing the Internet via a wireless LAN, as the considerations for WLAN are slightly different. Nor would mobile Internet typically include non-Internet mobile data, such as short messaging service (SMS) for phones, or simple one-line pagers.

So what, one might ask, is the big deal about mobile Internet? Why is it important or different from the fixed Internet? There are three main differences between mobile and fixed Internet: a wider audience, a less standard platform, and more limited capabilities.

A wider audience

The mobile Internet has a much larger potential audience, in terms of users already comfortable with the device. At the end of 2001, there were approximately 1 billion mobile phone users in the world. Compare this with around 500 million Internet users, half of whom are active.

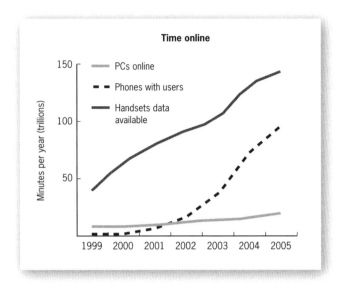

Figure 6.2 Devices and time online. (Source: D. Aron and J. Sampler)

Clearly, a mobile phone user is not necessarily going to convert to being a mobile Internet user, but nevertheless the figures are striking.

If we then compound the issue, by imagining how many 'user minutes' are available, in terms of users using their devices, the figures become more amazing. Although Figure 6.2 is a rough estimate, it is clear that we have our phones with us much more than we are sitting at our PCs, connected to the Internet. The inflection point in the 'Handsets Data Available' line represents the point that packet technologies, such as GPRS and PDC-P, begin to penetrate the market, heralding the 'always on' era, where as soon as a phone is switched on it is Internet accessible (unlike the GSM scenario, where the user must actively make a data call to be Internet-connected).

The technology challenges of the wider audience come from the fact that the device is always with the user – and the users cover a wide socio-demographic range, and the expectation is of an experience more like that of an ergonomically smooth consumer electronics appliance. Hence devices and services must be designed to be easy to use (without reading a manual), and services must be highly available (i.e. low downtime).

A less standard platform

Many people (including the authors) believe that the reason the Internet is so breathtakingly successful is that enthusiasts, academics, and military personal were able to build up a robust set of standards, which genuinely benefited everyone, before the big commercial players recognized the importance of the Internet and stepped in. The period of stability opening up the market, followed by unleashing the commercial drive of large companies, who were able to exploit the Internet for large profit, has resulted in incredible growth.

Many of the big IT companies were late in recognizing the importance of the fixed Internet, so they are all making sure that they are involved at an early stage in the mobile Internet, with conflicting stances, standards, and approaches. Companies such as Microsoft, IBM, Sun, Ericsson, Vodafone, and Symbian all have strong views and emerging product/ service lines for mobile Internet.

Most desktop users run a Web browser that speaks HTML (and normally DHTML, Javascript, and Java) using HTTP (and normally HTTPS) over a TCP/IP transport, has a screen capable of displaying colour pages of a similar resolution (VGA), and can support pages of any size. The mobile world, however, contains multiple markup and other languages (e.g. cHTML, WML, HTML, J2ME) using multiple session protocols (e.g. WSP/WTP, HTTP, i-Mode) over multiple transports (WAP, i-Mode), with many different screen sizes, graphic and colour capabilities, and many different memory capacities.

Also, the wide variety of underlying mobile networks, such as GSM 900/1800/1900 (Global System for Mobile communication), CDMA (Code Division Multiple Access), TDMA (Time Division Multiple Access), PDC (Personal Data Cellular), with newer technologies such as PDC-P (Personal Data Cellular-Packet), GPRS (General Packet Radio Access), EDGE (Enhanced Data GSM Environment), and CDMA2000 and W-CDMA (Wideband CDMA) emerging, makes for a challenging market for device vendors.

If we imagine a world with 3 device shapes (phone shape, palm shape, keyboard shape) × 3 markup language environments × 3 memory capacities × 3 session layers × 3 transports × 3 mobile networks, we have 729 different effective channels, before accounting for individual users' tastes (language, interaction style, topics of interest, time of day, etc).

This all adds up to a major headache for developers, who would ideally like to cater for all mobile users, ideally giving all of them the best

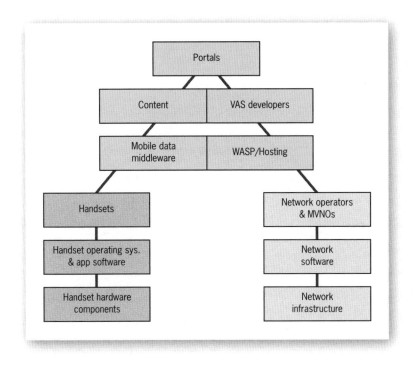

Figure 6.3 The mobile Internet value chain. (Source: D. Aron and J. Sampler)

experience they are capable of receiving, not a lowest common denominator service.

Further, for the same reasons as the technical diversity, the commercial environment for the mobile Internet is extremely complex. As Figure 6.3 shows, there is a complex value chain with eleven main classes of company involved in delivering a mobile service. A *handset* consists of various *hardware components* and *operating system and application software*. A *network operator, or virtual operator (MVNO)*, requires specialized *network infrastructure*, and various enabling *software* in the network. Then *Value Added Service (VAS) developers* develop services using *content* provided to them, based on *middleware* that solves various technical problems, potentially hosted by a Wireless Applications Service Provider (*WASP*). Groups of services are often presented through *portals*. All of these players must be synchronized, technically and commercially, to deliver a quality user experience.

Examples of companies in each of the above categories are listed in Table 6.1.

Table 6.1 Mobile Internet players.

Category	Example Players
Handset hardware	Qualcomm
Handset operating system and application software	Symbian, Microsoft, Palm
Handset	Nokia, Ericsson, Motorola, Palm, Panasonic, RIM
Network infrastructure	Lucent, Nortel, Ericsson, Nokia, Siemens, Marconi
Network software	Geneva Technologies (billing)
Network operator/MVNO	Vodafone, T-Mobile, TIM, Telefonica, Virgin, Debitel
Mobile data middleware	Kecrypt (security), Intuwave (fat client)
WASP/Hosting	Aspective
VAS application developer	Digital Bridges, Cybird (games), Peramon (B2E)
Content	Streetmap (location-related), Yahoo
Portal	Zed, Genie, Vizzavi, Mviva, Yahoo mobile

A limited channel

Finally, the fact that all mobile channels, whatever they are, are more limited than the fixed Internet world, makes service design much more challenging. The typical limitations are slower, less reliable Internet connections, much poorer input mechanisms (i.e. keyboards), smaller, less clear screens, much less memory, and much less processing power.

This makes for a very demanding environment in which to create compelling services, and is perhaps the main reason why the mobile Internet has been disappointing for many so far.

It is interesting that many of the skills needed in the tiny environment of the mobile phone are similar to those used in the world of the home computer, which preceded the PC, where memory sizes of 16 KB and processing power of 1 MHz were not uncommon, compared with the 512 MB and 1 GHz of the current standard PC.

The following text box explores the reasons why i-Mode has taken off in Japan.

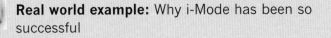

Real world example: Why i-Mode has been so successful

Hyped as the 'next big thing' in the IT world, mobile Internet has largely disappointed market expectations, everywhere except in Japan. In Japan, i-Mode has grown explosively. As Figure 6.4 shows, i-Mode has grown to over 32 million subscribers in the past two years. It has also contributed strongly to DoCoMo's profits – DoCoMo is the darling of the NTT group, reporting almost US$4 billion in net income in 2001. (However, it should be noted that DoCoMo is also incurring significant capital charges, which make true 'free cash flow' negative.)

DoCoMo have continued to innovate, launching Javaphones, video-phones, and a very early 3G offering called Foma. They have also invested in foreign markets to the tune of over US$10 billion, including invest-ments in US company AT&T Wireless, Hong Kong's Hutchison, Hutchison

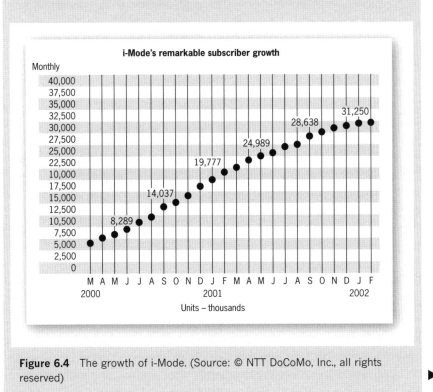

Figure 6.4 The growth of i-Mode. (Source: © NTT DoCoMo, Inc., all rights reserved)

Real world example *Continued*

UK, and the Netherlands' company KPN, in a move to proliferate i-Mode and W-CDMA, DoCoMo's 3G transport of choice.

There has been much speculation as to why i-Mode has rocketed, whereas WAP has not. This is largely attributable to the following four reasons:

1. DoCoMo are by far the dominant mobile network operator in Japan, and as such have been able to dominate the value chain, dictating standards and strongly influencing both handset manufacturers and content providers, effectively controlling the user experience.

2. Unhindered by standards committees, with their attendant complex politics, DoCoMo were also able to move fast in implementing solid technology. This resulted in much faster adoption of a packet network (PDC-P), a better security model encouraging genuine m-commerce (including banking and share trading), and continual innovation in phone and network capabilities, including videophones and Java phones.

3. In Japan, fixed home Internet connections are more costly, and consequently have lower penetration than in other markets. It is noteworthy that this market is controlled by NTT, DoCoMo's parent company.

4. Evidence suggests that, in general, the Japanese are strong early adopters of new technology. And despite recent economic difficulties, Japanese people still have significant disposable income.

In their vision presentations, DoCoMo do not see their growth as slowing due to a saturation of mobile phones. In contrast, they present a picture of everything that moves or is untethered having i-Mode connectivity, including vehicles and pets!

Mobile Internet communications technologies

The mobile Internet is a complex world of layers and protocols. As Figure 6.5 shows, there are essentially three layers to be considered. The lowest layer is the digital mobile telephony standard, used for all cellular applications on a network, whether they are voice, paging, or data. The middle layer is the wireless data standard, which consists of the

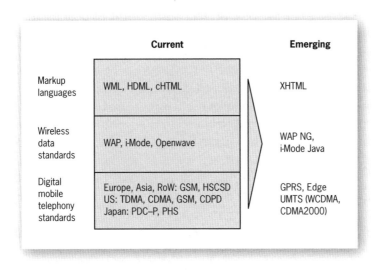

	Current	Emerging
Markup languages	WML, HDML, cHTML	XHTML
Wireless data standards	WAP, i-Mode, Openwave	WAP NG, i-Mode Java
Digital mobile telephony standards	Europe, Asia, RoW: GSM, HSCSD US: TDMA, CDMA, GSM, CDPD Japan: PDC–P, PHS	GPRS, Edge UMTS (WCDMA, CDMA2000)

Figure 6.5   The layers of the mobile Internet.

protocols layered on top of the digital telephony standard to facilitate mobile Internet sessions. The top layer in the chart is the markup language layer, consisting of the languages and environment used to describe content.

Digital mobile telephony standards

At the mobile telephony layer, the dominant standards in the Americas are CDMA and TDMA with some GSM. In Japan, there are multiple networks, but NTT DoCoMo, the leading player, uses PDC-P at present. In Europe, Asia (excluding Japan), and the rest of the world, GSM is currently the dominant standard. There is also a variety of other protocols used for pager networks, such as Mobitex and CDPD (Cellular Digital Packet Data).

These first standards of digital mobile telephony are often referred to as 2G, or second generation. (First generation refers to the increasingly unimportant analog mobile telephony standards, such as AMPS – Analog Mobile Phone System.) 2G technologies typically support fairly low data rates, such as 9.6 kbps. HSCSD (High Speed Circuit Switched Data) is an extension of GSM that some operators have implemented (such as Orange in the UK), giving speeds of up to 57.6 kbps.

There are three exciting ways in which the world of digital mobile telephony standards is developing. The first is the introduction of packet technologies. The second is increased data speeds. The third is global harmonization of standards.

2G networks (e.g. GSM, TDMA, CDMA) use circuit switched data. This means that, when mobile phone users want to have a data session, they have to make a mobile call for the duration of their data session. A better alter-native is packet data. In a packet data environment, as soon as a mobile phone is switched on, it is Internet connected and has an IP address. This means that push modalities become possible, where information can be pushed to a mobile user. It also means that the charging basis changes from time connected to a 'per packet' or a 'per megabyte' basis. GPRS is an early example of a packet technology, with the potential to offer maximum speeds of over 100 kbps. At the time of writing, it has been deployed in a limited fashion by some mobile operators. One issue holding back GPRS is finding an appro-priate charging scheme, which is simple enough and 'fair' to the cus-tomers. This first generation of mobile packet data standards is referred to as 2.5G.

The first 3G networks were launched in Korea and Japan in late 2000 and early 2001 respectively. It is expected that most major operators will roll out their first 3G networks in 2002–3. 3G refers to the next genera-tion of digital cellular networks, with much higher speed packet data than available in a 2G world.

There is no universally agreed definition of 3G, but the IMT-2000 standard, defined by the International Telecommunications Union (ITU), is perhaps the best proxy available. IMT-2000 defines a require-ment for packet data speeds of 144 kbps in wide areas, 384 kbps in urban areas, and 2 mbps inside buildings or in fixed applications. It defines five 'modes' of reaching this requirement, the two most signific-ant being CDMA2000 and W-CDMA.

The Americas, Korea, and some other countries are focusing on CDMA2000 networks, and Europe, Japan, and much of the rest of the world are focusing on W-CDMA. For the CDMA2000 camp, there are multiple steps on the way, starting with CDMA 1x (RTT), followed by CDMA 1x EV-DO, CDMA 1x EV-DV, and later CDMA 3x. For the W-CDMA camp, the evolution is GSM, GPRS, EDGE, W-CDMA. The 3G vision for the GSM world is also known as UMTS, the Universal Mobile Telephony Standard.

Table 6.2 Mobile digital telephony standards.

	Theoretical Max	Always On	Deployed
GSM	9.6 kpbs	No	Now
HSCSD	57.6 kbps	No	Now (patchy)
GPRS	115 kbps	Yes	Now
EDGE	384 kbps	Yes	Unclear
3G (IMT-2000)	2 mbps	Yes	2002–3

This seems like a maze of acronyms, but, essentially, each camp is evolving to a standard that meets or exceeds the IMT-2000 requirements described above, and operators may implement, delay, or skip each of the stepping stones, depending on forecast economic cost/benefit analyses. Given the amount that operators have had to spend on 3G licences ($66 billion in the UK, France, and Germany), and the current state of the global economy, it seems likely at this point that operators will choose to minimize the number of changes to their cellular infrastructure.

Characteristics of these technologies are summarized in Table 6.2. Appendix II has a detailed list of network communications speeds. There are also many good summaries of the characteristics of each of the above stepping stones on the Web, including Qualcomm's and Ericsson's Web sites.[13]

3G trials in Japan and the Isle of Man proved somewhat problematic, and it is expected that 3G technologies will take some time to fulfil their promise, due to issues with frequency bands, roaming, and battery life.

Figure 6.6 provides an interesting view of what different data speeds allow users to do. Note that the scale is logarithmic, so, for example, while it would take about 7 hours to download a 10-minute movie clip to a GSM device, it would take between 2 and 10 minutes for a 3G device (depending on how close it came to the theoretical maximum), which means that video conferencing and streaming video are comfortably achievable if 3G even comes close to achieving its potential. As another example, a typical 3-minute MP3 music track would take 40 minutes to download to a GSM phone, but between 10 seconds and 1 minute on a 3G device.

---

[13] http://www.qualcomm.com/cdma/3g.html, http://www.ericsson.com/technology/

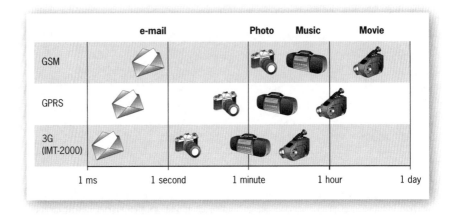

Figure 6.6 Implications of faster mobile data speeds.

Wireless data standards

In order to create an Internet/World Wide Web-like environment for mobile devices, a number of protocols are needed to handle session management, security, cookies, etc., just like the fixed Internet protocols discussed in Chapter 4 (TCP/IP, HTTP/HTTPS).

Wireless data standards have to take account of the wireless channel being less reliable, and hence have been designed a little differently from fixed protocols, with smaller packet sizes and different rules for detecting and fixing transmission errors.

There are two predominant standards in this area – WAP and i-Mode, plus some older standards from Openwave and others. Although they are converging, currently they each have their own solutions to the wireless data standard needs. For example, WAP has a session layer called WSP (Wireless Session Protocol – equivalent to HTTP in the fixed world), a transport layer called WTP (Wireless Transport Protocol – equivalent to IP), and a security standard called WTLS (Wireless Transport Layer Security – equivalent to SSL/TLS). There are also alternative approaches from others such as RIM (Research In Motion, who make the Blackberry interactive pager) and Pogo, a small UK startup.

What each of these standards has in common is the need for a gateway to convert between wireless protocols and fixed protocols, so that mobile devices can access services on standard Web servers, as shown in Figure 6.7.

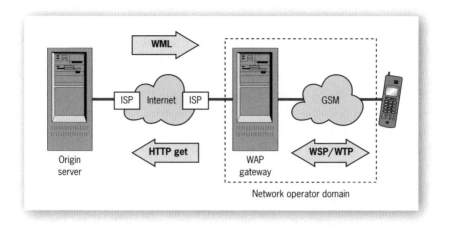

Figure 6.7 The mobile gateway – WAP example.

This mobile gateway has two commercial implications. First, there is an opportunity for the owner of the mobile gateway (normally the mobile network operator, such as Vodafone) to control access to the Internet, creating what has been dubbed a 'walled garden'. Secondly, this creates extra security considerations for sensitive services, such as mobile banking.

The walled garden debate continues, with most feeling that any attempt to limit Internet access from phones will ultimately fail. In practical terms, it seems as if operators may not limit Internet access, but will make access to preferred partners' content and services considerably easier, through the use of friendly menus, as NTT DoCoMo have done with i-Mode.

The security issue is not present for i-Mode, as the security model used is completely compatible with the fixed Web, and, while there are currently proprietary solutions for the 'WAP gap', as it is known, future versions of WAP will include standard solutions to the problem.

The Open Mobile Alliance (previously the WAP Forum) is responsible for the WAP standard. NTT DoCoMo own the i-Mode standard. Both are continually improving their protocols and content environments (see next section), influenced politically by their key members. Openwave's technologies were the foundation for WAP, and are less and less relevant over time.

Content markup languages

i-Mode uses cHTML (compact HTML), a subset of the Web language HTML. Current versions of WAP use a markup language called WML (Wireless Markup Language). Openwave's standard includes HDML (Handheld Device Markup Language), very similar to WML.

It is argued that one of the reasons that i-Mode is so successful is that many Web services work automatically on i-Mode phones, as the HTML they use is compatible with cHTML.

As Web content and services are migrating to the XML standard, it seems increasingly likely that mobile and fixed devices will use XHTML (Extensible HyperText Markup Language), an XML-compliant language, as their display language of choice. New versions of WAP are based on XHTML.

There has also been a significant movement to create Java environments on mobile devices, allowing Java applets to run on phones and WIDs. Current i-Mode phones have a limited Java virtual machine (JVM) on them, and Sun's mobile vision, J2ME (Java 2 Mobile Edition) with a smaller JVM, called a KVM (K Virtual Machine), is increasingly compelling.

This means that quite sophisticated programs will be downloadable from the Internet to mobile phones and WIDs, including business applications, personal information management, and games.

It is likely that most mobile devices will support both XHTML content and Java applets by 2004–5.

Messaging standards

Note that, as well as mobile Internet access, most phones have a much more lightweight messaging capability – the most popular one being SMS, the Short Messaging Service. Although it is very simple in its capabilities (around 160 text characters per message), SMS is the real mobile data success story to date, as it is so easy to use. In December 2001, for example, there were around 1 billion SMS messages sent per day globally.

More recently, SMS was extended to EMS (Enhanced Messaging Service) giving it slightly richer capabilities, but more significantly, towards the end of 2002, many operators launched MMS (Multimedia Messaging Service). MMS allows small pictures, animations, and audio clips to be downloaded to mobile phones, in a similar way to SMS. MMS

Figure 6.8 An MMS phone (Nokia 3650). (Source: Nokia)

is exciting, primarily in the consumer markets, as a much richer, but still relatively simple, messaging platform. Figure 6.8 shows an example MMS phone.

Architecture of the multimodal Internet

The challenge

The Internet has been an extreme test of computer architectures, in terms of capacity, scalability, and reliability. Until the advent of the Internet, computers needed to process at very high speeds, but did not need to handle hundreds of thousands, or even millions, of users. Not only do Internet-based solutions need to be able to handle large numbers of users, ideally they need to be able to scale up and down, to match costs with revenues.

Also, because Internet solutions represent a brand online, reliability requirements are paramount. This means that services have to be online, have a reasonable response time, and maintain clean, accurate data.

These demands have then been compounded by the addition of mobile and other 'multimodal' access methods. Multimodality means that users can access a system from different types of device at different times from different locations. This, combined with pressure to personalize services to improve user experience and 'stickiness', has led to a demand for the ultimate customization, which can be summarized in the following equation:

$$\texttt{User-Experience = Service} \times \texttt{Device} \times \texttt{User-Preferences} \times \\ \texttt{Location} \times \texttt{Time}$$

Hence, we have an extremely demanding environment: reliable, high performance, highly customized services.

Current best practice

The old-fashioned way of designing a solution, as a single monolithic application program sitting on a single server that serves the user requirement, is inappropriate for multimodal Internet solutions for the following reasons:

First, a solution that is a single program that can only run on one machine is not scalable, as to be truly scalable it must be able to run on several machines at once, to allow the cost versus capacity decision to be liquid (i.e. the management can choose to increase or decrease the quantity of physical assets tied up in providing the service in fairly small increments, at relatively little cost of scaling).

Secondly, the solution must be able to be balanced across several machines for another reason: in order to provide a robust service that has no single point of failure.

Thirdly, the core logic of the program (also called the business rules) should really be separate from the management of user input/output (also called the presentation layer). This is because the presentation layer may need to change many times to incorporate new devices and user interface requirements in a multimodal world, and ideally the core logic should be isolated and protected from these changes in order to reduce complexity, bugs, and maintenance needs.

Finally, the database portion, the business rules portion, and the display portion of a solution should ideally be executed on separate machines, as the performance characteristics of these three portions are often different, and they should be separately scalable.

The corollary of these four issues is that the architecture known as Three-Tier (or Three Layer) Architecture represents current best practice

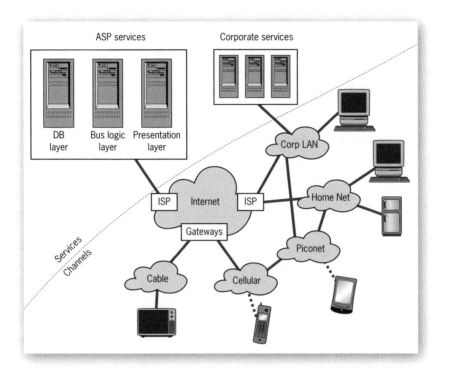

Figure 6.9   The multimodal Internet based on three-tier architecture.

for implementing Internet and/or multimodal service architectures, shown in Figure 6.9.

In a three-tier architecture, Database, Business Logic, and Presentation Logic are the three layers, and each exists as a separable layer. This enables these portions of the program to be scaled and made robust independently of one another.

To take an example of an online share trading service, the database layer stores the details of all customer holdings and transactions, and all the shares that may be bought or sold. The business logic layer has rules about who can buy how much of what, and what information is needed to complete a transaction, and the presentation layer deals with asking the user for input, and providing output to the user.

If such an online share trading service is designed initially with a Web-based interface, but using a three-tier architecture, it would be a relatively simple matter to add WAP and i-Mode interfaces, in order to allow mobile phone-based access, or even voice-based access using normal phones. Further, if new business rules arise, such as the need to warn buyers of insider trading regulations before making a purchase, the rule need only be inserted in the business logic layer once, and will work for all multimodal devices.

There are a number of tools and approaches to creating strong three-tier architectures, but probably the most powerful is a combination of J2EE, Application Servers, XML, and XSL.

J2EE, or Java 2 Enterprise Edition, represents Sun's vision of how to develop robust, scalable enterprise applications using Java. Among the components of J2EE are Enterprise Java Beans (EJB) and Application Servers. Without delving too much into detail, if a program is written using EJB, it may then be run in an environment in which an Application Server is running, and the Application Server will take care of scaling and robustness, by coordinating the program's execution across many machines.

Several companies offer Application Servers, the most prominent being BEA, IBM, Oracle, and iPlanet. Less commonly used ones include offerings from HP, Gemstone, JBoss (an open source group), Macromedia, and Orion.

For the display component, XML and XSL are often used. In this scenario, rather than the business logic layer producing user interactions in HTML, the language of the Web, it produces content in XML as input to the presentation layer.

As explained in Chapter 5, XML is a language for describing content, independently of how it will be displayed. XSL is a language for defining how content will be transformed for display. Hence a multimodal application using these technologies will generate XML descriptions of user interactions at the business logic layer, e.g. a share purchase confirmation in a stock trading service, then the presentation layer will transform those descriptions into either HTML (Web), WML (WAP), cHTML, or even voice 'pages', to be output to the user. Adding new device capabilities to an application involves changes only at the presentation layer, which might mean simply tweaking XSL rules. This combination of technologies makes for a powerful multimodal service architecture.

Finally, note that a general extension to the three-tier concept is '*n* tier'. An '*n* tier' architecture has each set of functionality that is logically separable, and with different scaling and robustness requirements is partitioned off into a separate tier.

Table 6.3 Mobile security technologies.

WiFi (802.11x)	Standard is WEP (Wired Equivalent Privacy). Many problems. Some proprietary solutions (e.g. 802.lQ) ASE (Advanced Encryption Standard) is proposed to fix
Bluetooth	Has proprietary security protocols – multiple modes. Frequency hopping makes hacking harder. Known problems with denial of service, strength of cipher, privacy
WAP	WTLS-used (similar to SSL). Problematic because of 'plaintext hole' at gateway. Proprietary solutions exist. WIM (WAP identity module) standard also available
i-Mode	Current generation uses SSL. More sensitive apps than WAP (e.g. mobile banking)
Mobile computing	Mobile-IP standard may be used to allow guest tunnelling through foreign networks

Security in the multimodal world

Security in the mobile/multimodal world represents an additional challenge, in that communication occurs in a more publicly accessible space, it does not always require physical connectivity, as the air is used as a medium, and furthermore there are many new protocols underlying wireless technologies, which are inevitably less mature, in a security sense, than fixed line standards.

Table 6.3 summarizes the current mobile technologies, and their unique security positions.

1. WiFi

WiFi, or 'Wireless Fidelity', is the alternative name for IEEE802.11b, the currently dominant wireless LAN technology. It is discussed in Chapter 8 as an emerging technology.

Radio wave transmission, as opposed to wired transmission, has different characteristics from electrical transmission down wires, the most notable being lower reliability/more chance of interference. Consequently,

Real world example: Drive-by hacking in London

In the 14 March 2002 issue of *Computer Weekly*, a UK IT trade magazine, a writer reported having been driven around the City of London by security consultancy I-Sec, with £500 worth of easily available equipment (amusingly including a Pringles tube as an arial). During their 20-minute drive, 49 WLANs were detected, 36 of which were not using any encryption (hence packets were readable), and 13 were using WEP encryption that was relatively easily hackable.

the protocols it uses need to be different from those used on the wired network, e.g. TCP. (Note that this applies to all wireless technologies.)

As security standards are strongly associated with transport protocols, each wireless standard has its own security solution. In the case of WiFi, the standard is WEP, or Wired Equivalent Privacy. At the time of writing, WiFi had many security holes, both in what could be achieved with best practice use of the technology, and in how the technology is typically deployed. These have been found and documented in many publicly available studies by universities and commercial research firms. For example, the above text box cites a 'drive-by hacking' test in London.

There are proprietary solutions available to secure WiFi WLANs now, and improvements in standards on the way, but in general WiFi technology is not yet secure as standard.

2. Bluetooth

Much of the above also applies to Bluetooth. However, Bluetooth was initially designed more for 'personal area networking'; that is, wirelessly connecting a person's phone, PDA, laptop, headset, and any printers or other peripherals in the area. This means that security was perhaps a lower priority in the minds of the founders of Bluetooth (largely mobile phone companies), but also that, for many applications, security is a little less critical, although one may also argue that Bluetooth is even more likely than WiFi to be used in a public area.

The bottom line is that strong security is also lacking in Bluetooth as standard, arguably even more in Bluetooth than WiFi, but we can similarly expect significant improvements over the next year or so, now that the technology is gaining some commercial acceptance.

3. WAP

WAP is the predominant mobile Internet standard for phones in Europe at present. Because WAP has a completely different stack of protocols from the fixed line Internet, it requires its own security standard, WTLS, or Wireless Transport Level Security. The currently deployed versions of WAP often face a security threat at the WAP gateway, where WAP protocols are converted to Web, as messages are converted between WTLS encryption and Web (SSL) encryption. This 'plaintext gap' is a cause for concern, as the owner of any service, e.g. online banking, would have to be happy that the gateway environment, normally owned by a mobile phone operator, is as physically and electronically secure as the service's back-office systems.

This 'WAP gap' has slowed the implementation of highly commercially sensitive services, like online banking and share trading. Proprietary solutions already exist, and newer versions of WAP address the problem.

4. i-Mode

Because its security technologies are highly compatible with standard Web technologies, i-Mode's security considerations are essentially similar to those for any Web environment.

i-Mode users have, however, been subject to e-mail viruses and also a great deal of spam (i.e. unrequested and unwanted) e-mails. The spam e-mails are particularly problematic in an i-Mode environment, as users pay a small amount for every mail that they receive. NTT DoCoMo have taken a hit of over US$200 million annually related to resolving this issue to their customers' satisfaction through pricing changes.[14]

5. Mobile computing

IP, or Internet protocol, was designed with the fundamental assumption that computers were static, i.e. a computer always connected to its corporate network and the Internet from the same place. This meant that it could have a specific IP address, and connect in from the same IP 'subnet' every time.

However, in a mobile world, an IP device, be it a laptop, WID, PDA, or data-enabled phone, requires access from different entry points at

---

[14] Source: 'NTT DoCoMo pays $217m to put spam back into the can' www.theregister.co.uk, July 4, 2001.

different times to its corporate services, and to the Internet. This means that standard IP protocols are not sufficient.

Mobile IP is the solution of choice for this problem, and will be a part of the global 3G offering. Mobile IP has a 'home agent' which sits on the device's home network, receives all packets destined for a particular mobile device, and tunnels them securely to that device, wherever it is connected.

Management perspectives

Mobile technologies were subject to a great deal of hype at the end of the dot com boom, and since then have suffered from the disappointment of reality kicking in. Nevertheless, mobile has significant value if applied judiciously. The questions for managers to consider are as follows:

- For my business, what real value can mobile technologies currently deliver, given existing technical limitations and constraints? What has been proven and what is marketing hype?
- Which applications would add most value to my business? This includes both B2E (Business to Employee) and B2C applications. B2E opportunities include mobile e-mail, diary and contact management, and improvements in supply chain and logistics processes. B2C opportunities relate to value-added services delivered to customers over the mobile channel, such as informational updates and mobile ticketing.
- How, if at all, does the timeliness and personal nature of the mobile channel affect employee and customer relationships? Does this represent an opportunity for my business, or a burden?
- What are the risks associated with mobile applications, such as damage to customer relationships, and extending the corporate security perimeter into the airwaves?
- In the next 2–3 years, what changes are likely to occur in the mobile arena? What additional opportunities and/or threats will these allow my business?

The future of IT

Concepts covered in this chapter

■ The three areas of IT progress: power, intelligence, and reach
■ The nine dimensions of technology progress: processing, storage, bandwidth, connectivity, user experience, commerce, languages, architectures, and algorithms

A question to ponder before reading

■ What are the different factors that have driven, and continue to drive, the value of IT to the corporate and consumer world?

A framework for understanding IT progress

Newspapers and other media are full of stories about different techno-logy advances, all couched in euphoric terms. For the average non-technical person, or even for many IT specialists, it is difficult to make sense of how significant advances like optical switches, new compression technologies, or even electronic fragrance emitters are.

The following is a model of the overall progress of information and communication technologies. Using three major dimensions (shown in Figure 7.1), split into nine minor dimensions (shown in Figure 7.2), the model provides a space in which all genuine IT advances can be mapped.

Every computer solution involves a computer of a given power using software algorithms of a given intelligence reaching a given number of users over given channels. Improvements in that solution stem from

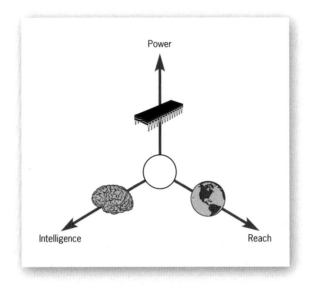

Figure 7.1 The three dimensions of IT progress.

improvements in one of these dimensions. For example, for an online banking system.

Improvements in power result in either more transactions being supported by a given hardware cost (sometimes called 'bangs for the buck', or better user experience (such as faster transaction turnaround time).

Improvements in intelligence allow given hardware to provide better performance through better software/algorithms, resulting in either more efficient (faster) transactions or more sophisticated functionality (e.g. learning users' preferences). Improvements in reach mean that either more users have access to the system (e.g. users with cable-TV Internet access only), or users have access from more places (e.g. mobile phone access as well as PC), or users have more friendly access (e.g. English language speech access to the system).

Every information and communications technology advance fits into one or more of these categories. More specifically, every advance fits into one of the nine categories in Figure 7.2.

1. Power/Processing

The CPU is the heart of the computer, and clearly, for any computationally intensive task, the speed of the CPU is critical. Data transformations

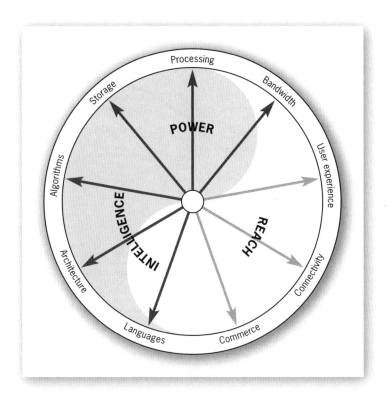

Figure 7.2 The nine dimensions of technology advancement.

such as sorting and file format conversion, as well as multimedia tasks like the rendering of streaming video[15] and audio, tax processing power.

Thus the task of increasing the processing power of chips, and making many chips work together efficiently, is a primary concern of many commercial and academic R&D efforts.

Moore's Law, devised by Gordon Moore of Intel, was a reflection, in 1965, that the number of transistors that could be packed into a given size of integrated circuit (IC) was doubling every 12 months. In 1975, he modified this to 18 months.[16] This means that chips can run twice as fast,

---

[15] Although the processing power needed to render video is often taken care of by a graphics co-processor board.
[16] There is some debate about whether the figure was 18 or 24 months.

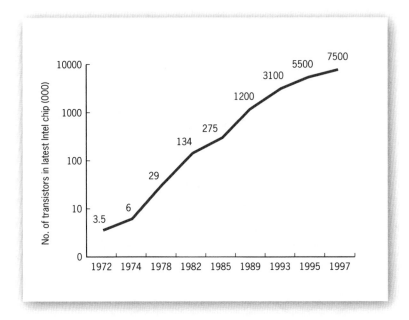

Figure 7.3 CPU power over time. (Source: Computer Electronics Manufacturers Association)

with twice as much complexity, potentially resulting in a 4 times multiple of performance. So far, he appears to be right.[17] See Figure 7.3.

At present, it appears that low-level physical limitations will make Moore's Law cease to apply in a few more years. However, there are many innovative R&D activities that may result in continued explosive growth of processing power, including 'biological computing' and 'quantum computing', which change the fundamental unit of processing from electrons to DNA and quantum states respectively. Also, the advent of '3D' chips, which build layers of a processor vertically much more than ever before, creates 'CPU skyscrapers', capable of delivering much larger power in a given physical footprint.

---

[17] In his book, 'The Age of Spiritual Machines', Ray Kurzweil attempted to fit a fourth-order polynomial to a graph of performance of 49 computers from Babbage's Analytical Engine in 1900 to a Pentium II-based PC in 1998. He found that the fourth-order polynomial approximated a straight line very closely – suggesting that Moore's Law is accurate, at least for the last hundred years.

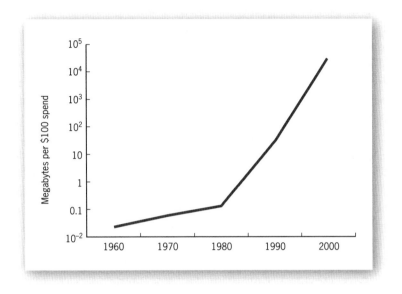

Figure 7.4   Storage capacities over time. (Source: Data Storage Institute, University of Singapore)

From the software side, advances in massively parallel processing (MPP) allow many, relatively inexpensive computers to work together on a solution, giving massive overall system processing power. It seems that one way or another, given the amount of global R&D, Moore's Law will continue to apply.

2. Power/Storage

Storage refers primarily to the memory on a computer and the hard disk storage within the computer. Storage too has gone through its own equivalent of Moore's Law, as Figure 7.4 shows.

As well as becoming larger, more sophisticated ways of connecting storage to computers and networks have appeared over time including RAID (Redundant Array of Inexpensive Disks – a method of using many small disks in parallel to provide faster, more reliable storage), NAS (Network Attached Storage – a method of attaching disks directly to a network rather than through a server, increasing reliability and speed of client access), and SAN (Storage Area Networks – allowing high-performance disks to be connected to several servers over a high-speed optical network.

Very recent developments include iSCSI, Infiniband, and storage virtualization. iSCSI is a method of making storage access inherently a more 'networked' operation, taking the SCSI format (Small Computer Systems Interface – a common way of attaching disks to servers) and packetizing the SCSI protocols, such that SCSI requests and replies can be embedded in IP packets, to increase flexibility of storage. Infiniband is a scalable, high-speed method of connecting computers to storage devices, being pioneered by Intel, among others. Storage virtualization refers to the concept of pooling many bits of storage around a network, or indeed the Internet, to create virtual disks that may be used by programs. The goal of this development is to abstract the location of storage from the applications that use it, having many potential benefits, including the ability for a network to move storage around intelligently, based on who is using it most.

Finally, a commercial development in the world of storage is SSPs, or Storage Service Providers. Consistent with the Internet services model described earlier, this class of business is designed to give corporate or individual users storage over the Internet. Providing the cost and availability of bandwidth is attractive relative to the cost of owning and managing storage in-house, and performance/latency is acceptable, this may prove to be a more mainstream business model in the future.

3. Power/Bandwidth

The third aspect of raw power of an IT solution is the speed at which components connect together. Connections from the home, from the mobile, from the office, and within the office are all increasing, and each one controls what is possible from each of these environments. Figure 7.5 shows the four types of bandwidth.

The home has experienced a revolution. Not long ago, the most common connection was a 9.6 kbps link to the Internet or the office. The only real practical use of such a link was for primarily textual content. Now, 56 kbps modems are commonplace, and many homes are making the transition to DSL and cable networks, offering speeds of several hundred kilobits to a couple of megabits per second. At these speeds, streaming video and substantial software downloads become feasible.

Within the office, LANs have moved from 10 Mbps to 100 Mbps as the common standard, with 1 Gbps used for aggregation of LAN segments, and 10 Gbps becoming available.

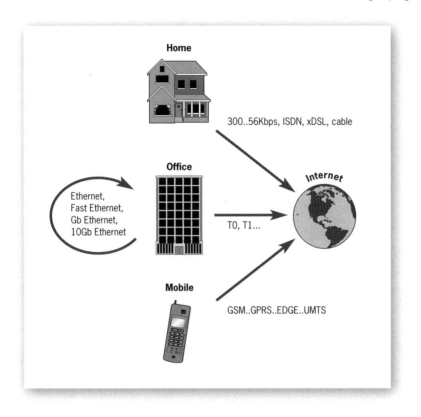

Figure 7.5 The four types of bandwidth.

Office-to-Internet standards, either for Internet access or VPN, have become a cost game. Infrastructure providers such as Global Crossing and Qwest have spent so much money laying cable during the dot com boom that it is not so much a question of what bandwidth is available, but more a case of 'how much money' for 'how much bandwidth'.

Mobile data is increasing in leaps and bounds, and is covered in detail in Chapter 6. It is interesting to note, however, in Figure 7.6, that there is potential for mobile Internet speeds to surpass those of fixed home connections in the next 3–4 years. It is by no means clear if UMTS will fulfil its 2 Mbps promise, but if it does we will be in the curious position where a user with an untethered laptop may be able to download data faster (if not cheaper) than with a desktop at home.

Other areas where bandwidth is increasing are in the connectivity of the disks to a computer (see previous section on storage), and from a

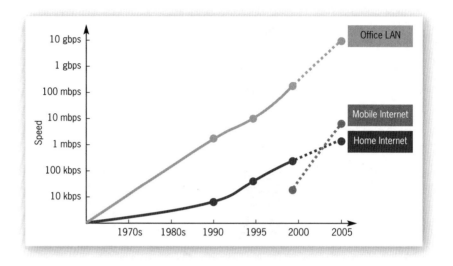

Figure 7.6 The evolution of bandwidth.

computer to its peripherals (printers, videocameras, scanners, etc). Peripherals are increasingly connected by USB (universal serial bus), and Firewire is popular for multimedia peripherals.

Overall, an important consideration going forward is the balance between server power and communications bandwidth. For B2B and P2P applications, simply the greater bandwidth the better, but for B2C applications bottlenecks may emerge. One hundred million users accessing a pay-per-view Web-based video server may experience much lower effective data transfer rates than their broadband connections allow, due to constraints at the server end. (Sad to say, but it is likely that, as with many other technologies, the pornography industry will be the first to experience these challenges, and the first to find a solution.)

Note that Appendix II contains a detailed list of bandwidth capabilities.

4. Reach/Connectivity

As mentioned in the networking chapter, Metcalfe's Law states that the value of adding a node to a network increases exponentially as the network becomes larger. This is quite intuitive in that, if you add a service to the network, the value is much bigger if there are more consumers of the service, and conversely it is far more exciting as a user to gain access to a network if it has many services on it.

The first generations of computers were standalone. Then, as computers became a more widespread phenomenon in the corporate world, IT moved from being standalone computers with 'dumb' terminals, to inter-departmental networks, what we would now call LANs. Later, LANs connected together over private leased lines to form corporate WANs. The next extension was inter-company leased lines, called EDI (Electronic Data Interchange).

In general, most of the networking technology was proprietary, delivered by the large IT companies of the time, such as IBM and DEC.

In the 1990s, the Internet moved out of the academic and military worlds, to standardize all of this, with everyone using TCP/IP as the underlying transport and Web-type technologies to create intranets, and later extranets, along with the Internet. This has created a worldwide network of incredible power and versatility. The Internet reaches into the heart of most corporate environments, and into the PCs in most homes.

The next phase (currently under way) involves bringing several other environments into the Internet/Web sphere, including:

- untethered devices in the workplace (using WLAN technologies);
- mobile phones and wireless information devices (over cellular networks);
- home entertainment devices other than the PC, such as the TV and video;
- home white goods (such as washing machines, refrigerators, heating systems);
- home utilities (electricity and gas meters);
- factory networks and equipment (commonly using non-Internet technologies).

For each of the above environments (see also Figure 7.7), reeling them in to the Internet/Web world unlocks a great deal of value, allowing remote monitoring over the Internet, data/information sharing for learning purposes, and cheap, flexible inter-networking (Virtual Private Networks).

Each of these environments needs a 'killer app' or other catalyst to champion the cause, and slowly they are finding them. For example, for white goods, the reduced purchase price of Internet-able products, so that they can be remotely monitored, maintained and learnt about, provides direct value to customers and manufacturers, and hence is a clear

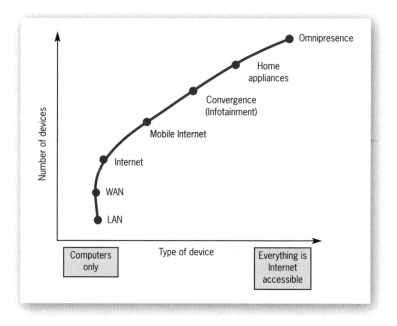

Figure 7.7 The evolution of connectivity.

win-win situation. For untethered devices in the workplace, productivity gains come from unwired ERP in stock rooms, and cheaper office reorganizations, which both provide clear bottom-line improvements. The mobile phone world has been struggling to find killer apps, but ultimately well-executed, synchronized PIM (personal information management) apps, such as diary and address book management, should push connectivity from a corporate angle.

5. Reach/User experience

IT solutions can also be said to reach further if they are more accessible to users. This means a friendlier/more natural user interface. The more friendly and intuitive the user interface, the greater the population and the wider the sociodemographic spread that you will reach.

The user interface had very humble beginnings, using switches and buttons to enter instructions one at a time into a computer, and reading the output from lamps. The interface quickly moved to punched card input and line printer output, which was workable for early commercial applications.

Since the 1970s, computers with keyboards as input and screens as output have been fairly commonly available. This is in essence the input/output environment that users are still using today – the major innovation being the 'WIMP' environment. WIMP stands for Window, Icon, Mouse, Pointer, and is pretty much equivalent to what is called GUI (graphical user interface) today. It was invented by Xerox in the 1970s and first popularized by the Apple Macintosh in the early 1980s, but normal personal computers were not really powerful enough to handle windows smoothly until the 1990s.

In the last few years, graphics have been improving constantly, and multimedia applications, such as Webcams and video conferencing, have been more possible. However, for IT solutions to penetrate much further into our lives, a much greater transition is needed. The paradigm needs to be reversed. Instead of the user needing to enter and learn about the computer's world, the computer needs to enter and learn about the user's world. The ultimate goal is what Don Norman (ex-Apple) calls the 'Invisible Computer', an environment where the users are no longer aware that they are interacting with a computer. For an IT systems interaction to feel completely 'natural', the input/output must be both more intuitive and more encompassing.

Figure 7.8 shows the evolution of the user interface along these two dimensions. Steps along the way include improved screen technologies such as electronic ink, 'artificially intelligent I/O' such as speech input-output and image recognition, virtual reality, and wearable computing. All of these applications are very processing-intensive, and, while all of the above have had some success in the laboratory, and possibly even a little commercial use, they are all still a long way from general purpose commercial use.

6. Reach/Commerce

Along with connectivity and user experience, the level at which one can conduct commerce over the Internet or other digital networks is a governer of the power of IT solutions. For a channel to be usable for commerce, it has to be available, reliable, and secure. For all three of these dimensions, perception/confidence is as important as reality. It is interesting in this context to compare the security of giving a telephone operator your credit card number verbally versus electronic transactions. Nevertheless, for a channel to become widely used for commerce, both the reality and the perception of availability, reliability, and security have to be achieved.

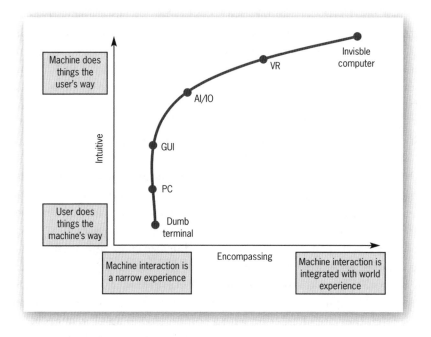

Figure 7.8 The evolution of the user experience.

The Internet was designed originally for informational, not transactional, purposes, and hence it has been necessary to establish a whole range of transaction and security standards, as well as addressing quality of service and reliability issues, in order to convert it, and other channels, to transaction-supporting ones.

Over the past 20 years, e-commerce has been growing both in scope and in spontaneity, as shown in Figure 7.9. The scope has moved from intra-departmental transactions, through inter-departmental transactions, through EDI, to B2C transactions and B2B marketplaces. There are also a number of P2P (person to person) models emerging. This move has taken the potential market of an IT service from a few users prepared to pay a small amount of their infra-structure budget, to around a billion users with trillions of dollars to spend.

The increase in spontaneity means a less planned transaction space. EDI (Electronic Data Interchange) represented the first inter-company model, with proprietary software and communications technology running over a private leased line, allowing two companies who had agreed several months before rollout to transact, and thus being able to perform

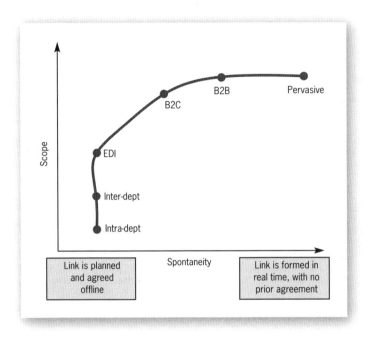

Figure 7.9 The evolution of e-commerce.

agreed transactions over the link. In a B2B marketplace, companies that have never met or communicated before (either in person or electronically) are able to buy and sell goods and services to each other, with the payment taking place electronically, and, if the good is informational, the transfer of ownership also taking place electronically. This spontaneity is fundamentally enabled by the proliferation of standards for connectivity, security, and presentation, in particular IP/HTTP, SSL, and HTML/Javascript/Java.

The future for e-commerce lies in three areas:

1. The rollout of similar transaction standards to new types of devices and networks entering the Web world (as explained in the Connectivity section above).
2. The continued strengthening of security and reliability standards to ensure that, as more and more transactions take place over the Web, the user experience remains attractive, and the cost/difficulty of electronic fraud remains higher than the value of perpetrating that fraud (through stronger encryption, better user identification, etc). IPv6 (Internet Protocol Version 6) is a significant emerging standard here,

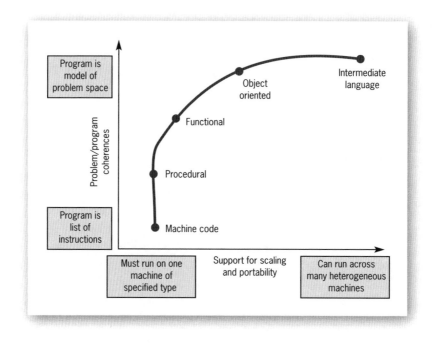

Figure 7.10 Improvements in computer languages.

supporting stronger security, as well as a larger number of Internet nodes, and support for streaming media such as video.
3. Standardized support for new economic/transaction models that emerge over the Web, such as those that aggregate buyers for increased buyer power.

7. Intelligence/Languages

By empowering the developer with a higher layer of abstraction, the evolution of computer languages makes new applications practicable that were simply too complex to consider earlier, and makes applications in general more reliable and scalable.

It is useful to think of progress with computer languages in two dimensions. The first is the coherence of the program with the real world that it is representing. The second is infrastructural support for scaling, portability, and robustness. These are shown in Figure 7.10.

The common computer languages are discussed in detail in Chapter 3. The move from machine code through to object-oriented environments has represented a massive advance in problem/program coherence

– meaning that the program looks much more like an explanation of the world it is representing than simply an obscure recipe to make a computer do something that is useful. As explained in Chapter 3, this results in a program that is much easier to maintain, change, and extend as the real world requirements change.

Perhaps reflecting the commercialization of the Internet, much recent work on computer language has reflected increases along the second dimension, support for scaling and portability. The Java J2EE environment and the Microsoft .NET environment are both attempts to make it very easy to develop highly robust, scalable Web services.

It can be expected that the next few years will be about bedding down this second dimension, with little fundamental change in languages. Arguably one of the downsides of the massive popularization of IT is that much R&D effort is diverted to more commercially oriented and slightly shorter-term research.

8. Intelligence/Architecture

Architectures, in a software sense, refer to the structure of programs, and what they can rely on underneath them in the IT environment in which they will be run.

Broadly speaking, to date, architectural improvements have helped in two ways: the first is allowing programs to abstract away from detail, and the second is the decoupling of pieces of a program, to allow simpler maintenance and separate performance management, tuning, and scaling of components of an IT solution. This is shown in Figure 7.11.

In the early days, there was no real software architecture – a computer ran the program you told it to, and that was it. Any work that needed to be done was written into your program, and there was no decoupling of components, as there was only one component.

The first real step to architectures was the creation of operating systems, such as Microsoft's MS-DOS. These operating systems ran 'underneath' any user program that was running, and allowed that program to call its functions, which performed low-level tasks, such as controlling the screen, driving printers, and structuring files on a hard disk drive. This allowed the programmers to concentrate on their application's business functionality, and ignore the details of how to keep the disk structured, the peripherals happy, etc.

The next major step was the introduction of multi-tasking operating systems, which allowed many programs to run at once, sharing the

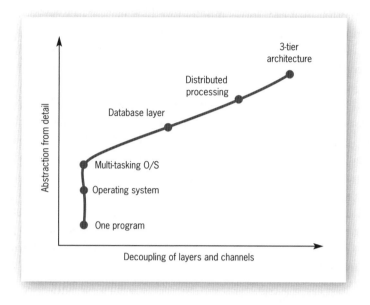

Figure 7.11 The progress of computer architectures.

processor. This development generally went hand in hand with the introduction of window-based graphical user interfaces (GUIs), so that the
output of several programs could be seen at the same time. Microsoft
Windows™ was an early example of a multi-tasking GUI-based operating system.

After that, the introduction of a separate database layer was a significant development, separating the database, which typically has different
performance and reliability characteristics, from the application, again
relieving the burden of data organization and integrity management from
the programmer.

Another sophisticated architectural ploy was the introduction of standards to facilitate distributed processing. These standards allow different
parts of a program to be spread across different physical computers,
invoking each other and synchronizing with each other at appropriate
times. An early standard for distributed processing was Remote Pro-
cedure Calls (RPC), and a popular standard compatible with the object-
oriented language paradigm is CORBA – Common Object Request Broker
Architecture – allowing different objects to sit on different machines.

New standards for passing data between programs are also helping
with distributed processing. As part of Microsoft's .NET initiative,

SOAP (Simple Object Access Protocol), based on XML, is a useful standard for passing information between distributed components.

Finally, currently in vogue is the three-tier architecture explained in detail in Chapter 6 in the section entitled 'Architecture of the multimodal Internet'. The bottom line of three-tier architectures is that data management, business rules, and presentation rules can be separated and individually managed, changed, and scaled. The benefits touted include reduced total cost of ownership, quicker development, better performance, and increased scalability. Like any new approach, it is taking a while to settle, such that all the benefits are fully realisable, but three-tier is very attractive for Internet-based services. A common set of standards for implementing three-tier architectures is Sun's J2EE. Also discussed in Chapter 6 is the extension of this concept to '*n* tier', where every separable set of functionality with different scaling and robustness requirements is partitioned into a separate tier.

9. Intelligence/Algorithms

Initial commercial computer applications used fairly straightforward mathematical functions, e.g. to calculate a company's payroll. Over time very robust, accurate, comprehensive libraries of mathematical functions developed, such as the NAG (Numeric Algorithms Group) library. These contained every type of arithmetic, trigonometric, matrix, and algebraic formula.

However, along with the growing complexity of conventional algorithms, researchers began to experiment with algorithms that were not conventional formulae, but were only possible on computers, such as neural networks and genetic algorithms. These algorithms, for the first time, represented a type of learning, even though that learning was fairly constrained.

Current research is moving towards more and more general learning, in other words algorithms that learn things the programmer did not tell them to learn. This type of algorithm will be needed to underpin very sophisticated natural language processing and robots. The evolution of complexity and learning aspects of algorithms is shown in Figure 7.12.

10. Non-technical drivers of IT progress

As well as the above nine technical forces, Figure 7.13 shows the non-technical forces driving improvement in information and communications technologies.

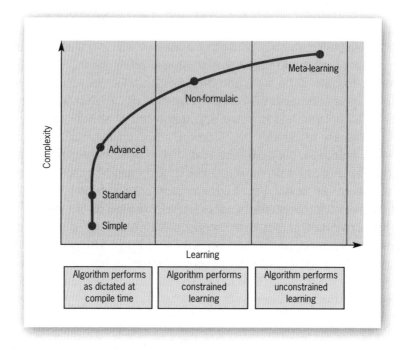

Figure 7.12 The evolution of algorithms.

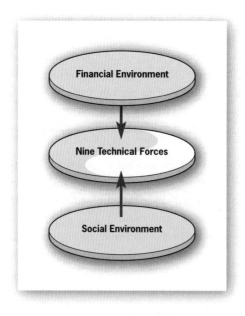

Figure 7.13 The non-technical drivers of IT progress.

These drivers fall roughly into two camps – the social environment and the financial environment. Social drivers include mass market acceptance of new technologies, overall levels of IT education and literacy, and financial affordability of technology. Increases in any of these forces creates a faster, more effective feedback loop for the productization of technology.

Secondly, sophistication of the financial markets, in terms of the availability of 'tech-savvy' financial institutions, such as venture capitalists (VCs) and banks, accelerates IT progress by starving startups with flawed business models of funds, and funding technologies with a great deal of potential, even if revenues are a long way off.

The recent dot com crash notwithstanding, it is in the second of these camps that North America has remained significantly above the rest of the world, with more sophisticated understanding of IT in financial institutions, and more specialized support services, financial and otherwise, for IT companies.

Management perspectives

In this chapter an integrated framework was presented to better understand the nature of technological advancement, as well as the forces driving it. The goal of the framework is to prevent technology advances from surprising you, coming at you from unexpected quarters. This framework leads managers to consider issues such as the following:

- Which of the nine factors in the model is accelerating, or slowing down the advancement of key technological changes in my industry?
- Are there any hidden dependencies between dimensions that make for complex adoption dynamics, e.g. the inter-relationship between CPU power and richness of user interface?
- Which of the nine forces can my firm control versus which can I not control? How can the uncontrollable risks be mitigated?
- How do I keep abreast of changes in these nine forces?

CHAPTER

8

The near future

Concepts covered in this chapter

- The xInternet and Web services
- Bluetooth personal area networks (PANs)
- Wireless information devices
- Artificial intelligence
- A description of UK intelligent software company, Autonomy
- Leading and bleeding edge technologies, including RFiD, biological and quantum computing, quantum cryptography, voice input/output, virtual reality, wearable computing, ubiquitous connectivity, any2any commerce

Questions to ponder before reading

- What is the xInternet/Web services concept that industry analysts are talking about?
- What is Bluetooth, and what does it do?
- What does artificial intelligence (AI) mean? What can AI do for us?
- What are the most interesting leading and bleeding edge technologies on the horizon?

Next, we highlight four emerging technology areas: xInternet and Web services, Bluetooth PANs, wireless information devices, and artificial intelligence.

Emerging technology 1: The xInternet and Web services

Despite the many and various extensions to the Internet and Web model, described in Chapter 5, there is a sense in which current Web technologies can be considered an early prototype – one could call it Web 1.0. The Web grew almost by accident, and the browser-based approach has proliferated like wildfire, but is nevertheless very limited.

Increasingly, IT vendors and industry analysts have been envisaging the next wave of the Web, dubbed the xInternet. Since it is a loosely shared vision, exactly what the xInternet refers to and contains varies depending who you talk to, but in general it addresses the following:

- *Identity*: The need for a user's identity, attributes, preferences, and permissions to be stored once in a secure and standard way, accessible to any service that requires identification or personalization.
- *User experience*: A much greater user experience, no longer tied to a browser, but more like normal applications (e.g. Microsoft Word) that have Internet components.
- *Multimodality*: A standard way of approaching the need for multiple device access.
- *Services not applications*: Rather than applications that you buy, install, and which then sit on your computer's hard disk, functionality will be delivered as services that you lease, delivered as ASP services, requiring connectivity.
- *Automated service discovery*: A standard way for devices and services to discover each other, and even negotiate for the best service, based on the user's preferences.
- *Intermittently connected applications (ICAs)*: applications on mobile devices that need to be able to perform standalone, then synchronize when connected (and possibly perform better when connected).
- *Spontaneous networking*: the ability for devices (usually wireless) to discover each other and work together automatically. e.g. a PDA and a printer in an airport lobby.

The large IT vendors each have their own branding, spin, and vision for the xInternet, to varying levels of completeness and focus. Microsoft's vision is .NET, while Sun's revolves around J2EE and J2ME, with other technologies such as One and N1.

Underlying technologies important in this area include XML, as a standard way of storing information in a self-describing way, and SOAP, a standard initiated by Microsoft for passing objects between programs. Microsoft are also promoting WSDL and UDDI as Web service standards for discovery and interoperation, and Sun have JINI and JXTA to achieve similar things.

.NET is perhaps the most interesting example of an xInternet vision, mainly because it comes from Microsoft, hence is bound to have significant impact on the IT world. Microsoft have long been at the centre of almost every PC in the world. .NET is their attempt to put themselves at the centre of the Internet.

.NET consists of three things:

1. A set of technologies that enable their vision of the xInternet, including the C# language, SmartTags, Information Agents, SOAP, WSDL, UDDI, and .NET versions of their Web and object components, such as ADO and ASP.
2. A set of core services that Microsoft and third party services can take advantage of/build on, covering Identity, Notification and Messaging, Personalization, Personal Information Management, and Dynamic Data Delivery.
3. The transition of many previously standalone applications to Web-based services, including Windows.NET, Office.NET, Visual Studio.NET, MSN.NET, bCentral.

It is both exciting and scary to think of Microsoft having every MS Office user around the world connected to their servers. Potential benefits in terms of piracy reduction, customer preference learning, and differentiated pricing are staggering. Potential loss of privacy and increase in Microsoft's power are a little daunting.

It is unclear exactly how the xInternet will emerge, but all the big players will be jostling for position over the next 3–5 years.

Emerging technology 2: Bluetooth PANs

The concept of a personal area network (PAN) has appeared over the last decade as a reality. The idea is that, once a person has several electronic devices with them, e.g. a mobile phone, a PDA or WID, a music player (Walkman, DAT, minidisc, MP3), a headset and/or microphone, they effectively become a walking network. Applications exist today for each of these devices needing to interact with at least one of the others. The ability to make those connections wireless is attractive for four reasons:

1. In order to get rid of the clutter of wires.
2. To allow more convenience, e.g. using a PDA to connect to the Internet through a mobile phone, while the mobile phone remains in your briefcase.
3. Where there is a need for more complex connections than one-to-one, for example if a headset is shared by a phone, a PDA, and a minidisc player.
4. Where one might want to communicate with another person's PAN, e.g. sharing contact or calendar details, swapping MP3 tracks, or spontaneously connecting to fixed devices in the local area, such as printers or Internet-connected PCs.

This area is just emerging, with many people carrying either no devices or only one, with very few requirements to interconnect them, until now. The need had earlier been satisfied either by a cable (e.g. Walkman to headset), or via infrared connection, for some phones and PDAs. The downsides of cables are obvious, and infrared is inconvenient, because, unlike radio frequency technologies, infrared requires 'line of sight' for connection. In the case of the common infrared standard IrDA (Infrared Data Association), this means that the two devices must be pointed at each other within a cone of 30°, and within about one metre of each other. IrDA is also a point-to-point technology, meaning that it is only appropriate for two devices communicating, not for a network.

Two radio frequency technologies have emerged to solve these issues and address all four of the above needs: WiFi (also known as IEEE802.11b) and Bluetooth. Both operate in the same RF waveband. WiFi comes more from the networking vendors, and Bluetooth more from the phone vendors. Hence the features of Bluetooth are a little more suited to PANs (lower power consumption, native ability to support spontaneous networking), while WiFi lends itself more to wireless LANs (higher speed, higher security, longer range, better for networking as opposed to point-to-point communications). The bottom line is that the smart money is on Bluetooth, shown in Figure 8.1, to dominate the PAN scene.

The current incarnation of Bluetooth allows a PAN, or in Bluetooth terms a Piconet, to contain approximately 255 devices, and for multiple Piconets to communicate as a Scatternet. The distance between devices must be less than 10 metres. This limitation is due to the very low power used in Bluetooth (1 milliWatt). A higher power version has been

Figure 8.1 Bluetooth headset. (Source: Ericsson)

specified with 100-metre range, but is not the predominant technology today. Bluetooth can transmit data at speeds of up to around 700 kbps, although real world research has shown speeds of around 50–300 kbps to be more likely.

As of late 2002, there were 580 products that officially conform to Bluetooth standards, ranging from the mobile phones and headsets from companies like Nokia and Ericsson, to Toshiba microwave ovens, refrigerators, and washing machines.

Applications of Bluetooth PANs vary from simple wireless headsets, through to automated PDA synchronization or wireless home networking. Real world applications of Bluetooth may suffer security issues and interference issues, as the Bluetooth signal is very weak, and operates in a radio band (2.4 Ghz) that is unlicensed in most countries, hence free for any device to use. Nevertheless, it is expected that Bluetooth PANs will increase vastly in number over the next five years, while WiFi and its extensions (802.11a and 802.11g) will similarly dominate in the wireless LAN area.

Emerging technology 3: Wireless information devices (WIDs)

The need for WIDs

To date, there have been three types of mobile device, in terms of computing and communications: mobile phones, personal digital assistants (PDAs), and laptop computers, shown in Figure 8.2.

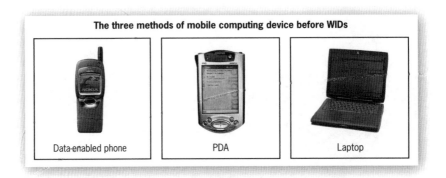

Figure 8.2 Phones, PDAs, and laptops. (Sources: Nokia, Compaq)

Mobile phones have been used primarily for voice applications, like making phone calls. They have obvious limitations as general purpose computing devices, in that the screens are small, and there is no good method of data input.

PDAs are traditionally centred around personal information management applications, like address book and calendar. They are limited by their lack of connectivity – they require connection to a mobile phone in order to connect to the Internet. And even when they have that connectivity, the voice and data functionality is very poorly integrated.

Laptops are cut-down PCs that are able to do everything a desktop can do, but are slightly less powerful (in terms of processing power per dollar). Laptops normally do not have their own wireless connectivity, and are also far too bulky/awkward to use in many mobile situations.

Hence, if one believes that there is value to be had in general purpose computing on the move, there exists an unfulfilled need for devices that work well in mobile situations.

The coming WID wave

The challenge is now on to find the devices of the future, that are not scaled-down PCs, or feature-phones, but that integrate voice and data, communication and computing, allow Internet connectivity, and effective input/output in a mobile context.

The first widely available device that could be called a WID (Wireless Information Device) was the Nokia Communicator (shown in Figure 8.3),

Figure 8.3 The Nokia Communicator. (Source: Nokia)

working innovatively as a simple phone when shut, but as a wireless Internet terminal when open.

A more innovative recent device is the Pogo, developed by Pogo Technologies, a spin-off of the 'new economy' consultancy, Razorfish. A Pogo is shown in Figure 8.4. Roughly the shape of a bar of soap, the Pogo is a mini Web terminal, with fully integrated GSM mobile telephone. Other than its highly innovative design, the other major innovation is the use of data compression to accelerate Web bandwidth. All Web requests from a Pogo device go through Pogo's servers, which use proprietary compression techniques to use much faster effective data rates over a standard GSM 9.6 kbps link. Further, telephony is fully integrated with data applications in the Pogo's software.

At the time of writing of this book, Pogo have achieved limited distribution with Carphone Warehouse in the UK, and their future is still in the balance.

Even the Pogo is a relatively conventional device, however, given the possibilities envisaged by some. Using alternative forms of input and output, and radically different form factors (i.e. shapes), experimental devices are being envisaged that fit much more naturally with human behaviour.

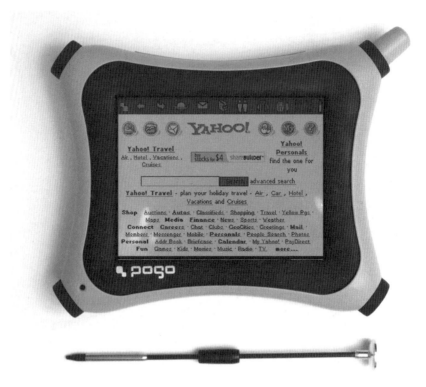

Figure 8.4 The Pogo WID. (Source: Pogo)

Figure 8.5 illustrates two concept devices developed by Therefore, a UK design consultancy, as part of some brainstorming work for the PDA maker Psion, before Psion pulled out of the consumer PDA market. The device on the left contains a camera in the centre, speaker, microphone and activation button, and a series of three screens that can be folded out like a deck of cards. The device in the centre is worn around the user's neck, with a projector in the left side projecting an image on to any flat surface, and a camera on the right side, enabling the remote party in a communication to see what the user can see. The simulation on the right shows this device in use.

Many of the more radical designs such as these are moving towards the 'wearable computing' goal, where technology can integrate seam- lessly into a user's mobile life. However, turning these WIDs into a com- mercial reality will involve advances in speech input/output, natural language processing, and various electronic components. It is likely that the next ten years will be very exciting ones for the evolution of the WID.

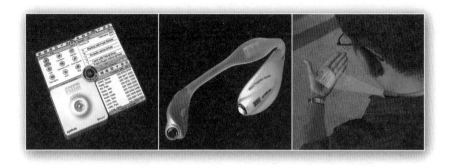

Figure 8.5   Therefore/Psion concept devices. (Source: Therefore)

Emerging technology 4: Artificial intelligence

What is artificial intelligence?

Artificial intelligence (AI) refers to computers performing anything that resembles human behaviour. It is not a hard and fast definition, but generally refers simply to computers doing clever things. AI has been a darling of the academic research world since the 1940s, as the problems involved in AI are so difficult and interesting, but more recently commercial applications have increased, as expectations have become more realistic.

Broadly speaking, AI can be broken down into two categories – 'humanlike' input/output, and computers working things out on their own. Humanlike input/output includes speech input, speech output, natural language processing, natural language translation (e.g. from English to French), image processing, image recognition, and virtual reality. The ultimate goal of humanlike input/output is for computers to operate in the human world, rather than, as now, for humans to have to operate in the computer world. Computers 'working things out on their own' includes advanced forecasting and pattern matching techniques, intelligent inferencing, and support for complex decision making.

Artificial intelligence technologies

Key technologies used for AI applications include neural networks, genetic algorithms, Bayesian statistics, semantic/pragmatic world models, expert systems, and fuzzy logic.

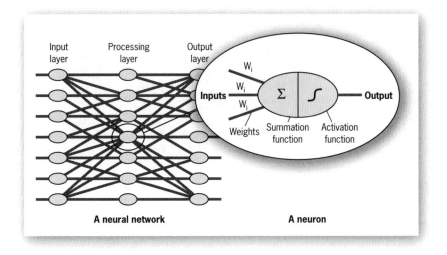

Figure 8.6 Neural network structure.

1. Neural networks

Neural networks (NN) developed from an attempt to model the way the brain really works, and are normally used for pattern matching applications such as fingerprint recognition, or forecasting applications such as program trading.

The fundamental unit of neural networking is the neuron. A neuron takes inputs, sums them up, and, if they reach an activation level, fires off an output, which may be connected to one or more neurons. Typically, neurons are organized in three layers – an input layer, a 'thinking' layer, and an output layer. For example, in a handwriting recognition system, the input neurons will correspond to the pixels on the screen where the signature is written, and the output layer would consist of either a single 'Yes' or 'No', or alternatively a probability of a match. The structure of a neural network is shown in Figure 8.6.

A network is initially built, then trained with a set of training data, for example a set of 300 signatures, and a 'Yes' or 'No' for each. In each training cycle, a signature is presented as input to the network, the output is observed, and, if the result is correct, the importance of the neurons that contributed to the right result is increased, and that of the neurons that detracted from the right result is reduced.

The training is repeated many times, until the network stops improving. The mathematics of neural networks is not fully understood yet, and also some are reluctant to use them, as there is no intuitive way to observe how they are achieving their results (i.e. there is no 'formula' to look at). However, practical application often shows stronger results than conventional predictive techniques such as linear regression, particularly in complex pattern matching applications like face, fingerprint, or handwriting recognition.

2. Genetic algorithms

Genetic algorithms (GAs) use the principles of Darwinian natural selection to find the optimal formula for forecasting or pattern matching. They are often a more effective alternative to regression-based forecasting techniques. Where simple regression can be said to be linear and parametric, genetic algorithms can be said to be non-linear and non-parametric.

For example, if we want to model movements in oil prices using external factors, in a simple, linear regression scenario we might create the formula 'oil price at time t = $coefficient_1$ × interest rate at time t + $coefficient_2$ × unemployment rate at time t + $constant_1$'. We would then use a metric such as 'ordinary least squares' to find the best set of coefficients and constants to model oil prices. There are two main issues with this approach. First that it is linear – in that we have made an assumption that oil price varies with interest rate, and not, say, interest rate squared. There is no reason to make this assumption, and what we would really rather be doing is searching through 'function space' (i.e. finding the best function of interest rate, whatever it is) rather than 'coefficient space'. The second problem is that we have determined which parameters to use (interest rate and unemployment rate) rather than searching through 'parameter space'.

Using a GA scenario, we would set up a meta-formula, or schema, saying something like 'oil price at time t is some function of up to 4 variables'. We would then provide data for a group of different variables, perhaps around 20. The genetic algorithm would then run, looking for the best function and the best variables. The way a GA works is deceptively simple, very intuitive, and strikingly similar to the way we believe animals to evolve.

Each formula that conforms to the schema given above is considered an individual in the population of possible formulae, much like, say, George Bush is an individual in the population of possible humans. The variables that determine any given formula are represented as a series of numbers, which make up the equivalent of the DNA of that individual. For example, the 'DNA' (0,1,4,6,7,3) may represent the formula 'oil price = gold price to the power 4, divided by the logarithm of the Nikkei index plus 3'.

The GA engine creates an initial population of formulae, maybe around 50 'individuals'. Each individual is tested against a set of test data, and the fittest ones, perhaps the top 10 per cent, survive. The rest are discarded. The fittest individuals form the basis of the next generation, and are mated together (swapping of elements of the DNA), and mutated (random altering of elements of the DNA).

By running through many generations, it is observed that GAs tend to create formulae that are more and more accurate. While neural networks are also non-linear and non-parametric, the great attraction of GAs is that the final results are more 'inspectable'. The final formulae will be visible to the human user, and conventional statistical techniques (such as standard deviation) can be applied to such formulae to give confidence levels of results.

GA technology is improving all the time, for example with the introduction of the equivalent of viruses (or apocryphal examples), which develop alongside the formulae designed to break the weak ones, and hence make the population as a whole stronger.

3. Bayesian statistics

Bayesian statistics is an area of statistics focused on estimating conditional probabilities, e.g. the probability that one event will happen, if another one does. Bayesian statistics has strong potential in the software world.

A recent example of the use of Bayesian statistics is for implicit personalization in the e-commerce world. Essentially, one may observe how a consumer behaves when looking through one's Web site, and from that infer topics of interest, preferred interaction style, etc. Recently sites such as Amazon.com have attempted to use this approach in combination with cookies to adjust their Web site automatically to be more appealing to the individual user. Clearly, if this goal is achieved, consumer 'stickiness' and loyalty are increased, switching costs are higher, repeat purchases should increase, and customer churn should decrease.

Another potentially powerful application for Bayesian statistics is the automated structuring of a large number of documents. By inspecting keywords within a document, it may be possible to infer the topics to

Key industry player: Autonomy

Founded in 1996 by Bayesian statistician Mike Lynch, Autonomy is a success story of the commercial application of an 'artificial intelligence' technology. The company's 1999 revenues were US$22 million, 2000 revenues reached US$65 million, and 2001 revenues were down slightly at US$52 million.

Autonomy's products are based around, and differentiated by, the intelligence of Bayesian statistics. Products include Profiler, which allows implicit personalization of a user's Web experience, and the Dynamic Reasoning Engine, for automatically structuring unstructured information.

Autonomy are building a wide range of Web software infrastructure products based on this platform, and have attracted quite a few blue chip clients, including Sun Microsystems, Telecom Italia, the BBC, Ericsson, and ABN Amro bank.

which they are most closely related. This is attractive for structuring documents within a corporate knowledge base, but may be extremely exciting for organizing the ultimate unstructured pile of documents – the Internet.

Autonomy – discussed in the text box on the next page – is a high-profile company which uses Bayesian statistics.

4. Semantic and pragmatic world models

Many of the great hopes of the AI industry, including true natural language discussions with computers, computer translation, and robotics, require the computer to have a measure of understanding of the real world.

A good example of this is considering difficult translation examples. For instance, to translate 'My name is Peter' from English to French requires no great real world knowledge – a simple set of rules to substitute French words for English could result in the correct translation 'Je m'appelle Peter.'

However, consider the paragraph, 'I asked the farmer where the sheep's feed box was. He told me that the box was in the pen.' In order to translate the second of these two sentences into French, it is necessary to understand that pen refers to an animal pen, not a writing implement. There are two possible ways to reach that conclusion – either by using the first sentence as context (i.e. we are in the farming world), or by understanding that boxes are normally bigger than writing implements.

A lot of less convoluted examples exist. The bottom line is that intelligent machines operating in the real world need some encoded understanding of that world with which to work.

Computational linguists normally describe interactions on four levels – lexical, syntactic, semantic, and pragmatic. In the context of human conversations, the lexical layer gives rise to letters and words. The syntactic layer adds grammar, allowing lexical elements to relate to each other. Semantics adds the concept of meaning, mapping grammatical structures to concepts of descriptions or events. Finally, the pragmatic layer is where meaning is given real world context. It is this layer, for example, that would contain the knowledge of the typical sizes of boxes and pens.

Lexical and syntactic analysis of human languages is relatively easy. Initial optimism about the capabilities of computers to translate language in the 1950s probably stemmed from the fact that researchers considered lexical and syntactic analysis to be all that was needed.

Building semantic and pragmatic models is a mammoth task, and to date the major successes have been achieved by focusing on very specific target areas, such as medical diagnosis or legal casework. At present a number of academic efforts are under way to encode as much semantic and pragmatic knowledge as possible, but it seems unlikely that significant commercial application of generalized semantic and pragmatic models will take place in the next five years. However, in specific vertical domains, such as medicine and law, models are already in successful use, and will continue to improve.

5. Expert systems

Expert systems are systems that encode a series of rules in a decision tree, which allows a computer system to make a decision much as an expert would. Typically, an expert systems engineer would spend time eliciting knowledge from one or more experts in a field (such as medical diagnosis), then encode those rules electronically, either within an expert system generation environment, or directly using a programming language such as Java.

A famous example of an expert system is MYCIN, a medical diagnosis system, which uses a series of rules to diagnose illnesses. An example rule from the MYCIN system is as follows:

```
IF infection is primary-bacteremia
AND site of culture is one of the sterile sites
AND suspected portal of entry is the gastrointestinal
tract
THEN there is suggestive evidence that infection is
bacteroid (70%).
```

As with natural language understanding, expert systems are much more successful when operating in very narrow domains, like diagnosing lung conditions or breast cancer in the medical fields, or property law.

6. *Fuzzy logic*

Fuzzy logic refers to systems that can work with varying levels of certainty, rather than just the 'TRUE' and 'FALSE' values that are more 'natural' in a digital environment. It has required the creation of a propositional calculus that is based on the concept of partial truth, extending functions such as 'AND' and 'OR'.

Fuzzy logic has been used successfully in expert systems, and other artificial intelligence applications, including control systems.

Current commercial applications of AI

After an initial period of excitement around AI in the 1950s, there was a wave of disappointment in the 1960s, as the vast amounts of research had provided little of commercial or real world value. However, research continued, and some technologies improved dramatically, resulting in useful AI applications such as speech recognition and remote medical diagnosis.

Further, people's expectations have been reset, and technologies that are far from perfect are being used to great advantage. The best example is Machine Translation (MT) of human languages. After accepting that high-quality automated MT is difficult, MT technologies have been developed to make human translators more efficient (rather than taking them out of the loop), and MT technologies are used to provide poor, but understandable, translations of content where users would not be prepared to pay for high-quality translation, e.g. the Babelfish translator of Web content, used by many search engines.

Another example is computer role-playing games, where computer 'characters' are imbued with an artificial personality. Released in 2001, the much touted game Black and White is a leading example here. This

Table 8.1 Prominent commercial applications of artificial intelligence.

Application	Technologies Used
Financial trading support/programme trading	Neural networks, genetic algorithms, non-linear dynamics
Biometric pattern matching, e.g. human face recognition, iris recognition, fingerprint recognition, handwriting recognition	Neural networks
Intelligent inferencing for implicit e-commerce personalization	Bayesian statistics
Automated content structuring	Bayesian statistics
Voice input/output	Text-to-speech, speech-to-text
Unified messaging	Text-to-speech, speech-to-text
Document summarization	Natural language processing, semantic/pragmatic world models
Language translation	Natural language processing, semantic/pragmatic world models
Decision support for medical, legal sectors, etc.	Expert systems, fuzzy logic

is a good application of current AI technology, as it is not so crucial if the technology is imperfect – i.e. it is not mission critical.

Table 8.1 summarizes some prominent examples of AI being used commercially. Other key applications of artificial intelligence are in the defence industry, in such areas as target identification and missile guidance.

Other leading and bleeding edge technologies

The previous section gave examples of technology advances that are either ready for commercial exploitation or close to it (e.g. ready within one year). In industry parlance, these represent 'leading edge' technologies.

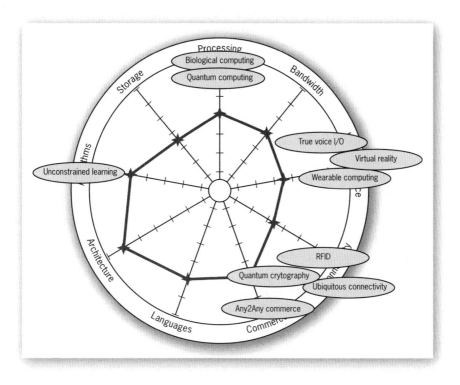

Figure 8.7   The bleeding edge of IT. (Source: D. Aron and J. Sampler)

Bleeding edge[18] represents technologies still firmly in the research lab-oratories, often in academic (as opposed to commercial) environments. The term 'bleeding edge' refers to the danger inherent in trying to com-mercialize them too soon.

Figure 8.7 shows nine key leading and bleeding edge technologies, which will have profound impact along one or more of the nine dimen-sions if they realize their potential, most likely in the next 5–10 years.

It is impossible to make a comprehensive list of all the bleeding edge technologies being developed today, but a few interesting ones are listed as follows:

---

[18] Note that the exact time horizon differentiating leading from bleeding edge varies widely. Some consider the newest versions of software, such as Oracle or SAP, to be bleeding edge because they need a year or so to settle, whereas the meaning we attribute to bleeding edge in this book is commercial viability within 5–10 years.

▪ RFID (Radio Frequency Identification), an innovative new approach to automatic identification and data capture. As a replacement for barcodes, RFID involves a tiny chip placed in an object or its packaging, with a reader used to track that object. Benefits include eliminating the need for 'line-of-sight' contact, the ability to scan many objects simultaneously, and the ability for objects to be scanned without any active effort. Applications vary from improved logistics and warehousing through to transport, ticketing, and payment. Although they are in use today, the cost of RFID chips needs to be driven down significantly from the current level of around $1 before they penetrate significantly.

▪ Biological computing, the use of DNA to perform calculations as an alternative to electromagnetic processors, which is interesting because it may be used to perform massively parallel computations. Biological computing has performed successfully in laboratory environments with very limited problems, the most famous being the travelling salesman problem (TSP), a computationally intensive optimization problem. One would suspect that this technology is at least 10 years away from commercial use.

▪ Quantum computing, the application of the principles of quantum physics to allow many different calculations to take place in the same physical space, increasing potential processor densities. Again quantum computing has had some success in controlled academic experiments, but is quite a long way from commercial application.

▪ Quantum cryptography, applying Heisenberg's uncertainty principle to encryption, such that passive snooping without being detected becomes impossible. This is also at the laboratory stage.

▪ True voice I/O, the ability to genuinely control your computer by voice, and receive output as speech. Current implementations of voice I/O from companies such as IBM, Philips, Lernout & Hauspie, Dragon Systems, and Nuance tend not to work well enough for general purpose operation of a computer. Clever algorithms and more horsepower are gradually assisting this process. Unlike the previous three technologies, this area seems to be experiencing slow improvement over time, as opposed to a sudden eureka.

▪ Virtual reality (VR), the collective name for techniques that feel more like interacting with the computer in the real world, rather than in the world of the computer. Examples include VR headsets, which create the illusion of a virtual world, or a virtual overlay on the real world. Very demanding in terms of processing power to give a realistic user experience, the majority of VR systems today are in use in military applications, but when the technology becomes more affordable this area holds great promise for many areas, including games such as flight simulators.

- Wearable computing, referring to technology that may be carried on the person in such a way as to be relatively invisible. This includes displays projected on to glasses such that the user has an 'augmented reality' experience, where digital information is overlaid on their view of the world. Although many of the core technologies exist today, size, battery life, and ergonomic complexity will probably prevent this technology from growing significantly over the next few years.

- Unconstrained learning, the ability for computers to learn things that the programmer did not envisage. This nirvana of AI/adaptive systems requires very comprehensive semantic and pragmatic views of the world. Probably the most famous commercial pragmatic world model at present comes from Cycorp, a company spun off from a large US R&D consortium. The 'Common Sense Knowledge Base' owned by Cycorp contains over 1 million hand-entered rules about the world. For example, a quote on their Website states that Cyc knows that trees are usually outdoors, that once people die they stop buying things, and that glasses of liquid should be carried right side up. When rule bases like Cycorp's become mature, many applications will be massively improved including natural language understanding and translation, robot behaviours, and adaptive control and safety systems in industrial environments.

- Ubiquitous connectivity, the capability of users to connect to personal, corporate, and public services wherever they are, whatever devices they are using, automatically roaming between whichever wired or wireless channels are cheapest, most reliable or most secure (depending on their preferences). This connectivity nirvana subsumes many changes and harmonizations in wired and wireless technologies, including home, office, factory, cellular, and metropolitan networks, with sophisticated spontaneous discovery and networking services, and commercially agreed standard mechanisms for negotiating rates. There are many pieces to this puzzle, all moving relatively fast, and we will slowly approach this goal over the next 5–10 years.

■ Any2Any commerce, the transactional equivalent to ubiquitous connectivity. Any2Any commerce implies secure, fast transaction capability (i.e. ability to buy or sell tangible or intangible offerings) between any two entities, whether they be individual users with WIDs or multinational companies. This includes B2C, B2B, and P2P modes. Also implied here is the ability to conduct any transaction modality electronically, including a simple purchase at a fixed price, a one-on-one negotiation, or an auction. Any2Any commerce is progressing well with new steps to the ultimate goal, such as secure mobile electronic wallets, appearing and becoming more standard every quarter.

Management perspectives

This chapter has described some of the potentially key evolving technologies. Issues for managers to consider here include:

■ What evolving technologies will most likely have a significant impact on my industry? In other words, where will key technologies be in the next 5–10 years, and what is the potential impact of this on current business drivers, e.g. industry structure, cost structure, customer reach, and sources of product/service differentiation?
■ What technical skills does my company have in these evolving technologies?
■ How much should we be investing in new technologies?
■ When should we be investing in these new technologies?
■ How do we stay informed of changes in new technologies? In particular, how do we remain informed about technologies making the transition from bleeding to leading edge?

Concluding thoughts

Armed with all of this technical knowledge, what should business leaders do next? First, and possibly most importantly, is a change in mindset and perspective. Senior management must realize that IT is not a department, but actually a perspective for business analysis. With this in mind, we suggest the following three-step programme as a starting point for using the information in this book:

1. Establish a technology audit process in your own firm, conducting periodic technology audits. Examine how technology is being used in your own firm and benchmark that against others in your industry. Examine not only what technology is being used, but how much is being spent (as a percentage of sales), the IT literacy of employees, and how the technology function is organized and managed in your firm.

2. Stay informed about new and emerging technologies. We hope this book has provided you with a good working knowledge of how IT works, as well as insight into some developing technologies. Unfortunately, technology is constantly changing. To keep abreast of this world, we offer several suggestions. First, read different publications. There are many magazines of differing types in this area. For example, most general business magazines have articles or columns dedicated to technology, e.g. *Business Week*, *Fortune*, *Forbes*, and *The Economist* have regular supplements on technology. There are specialist magazines describing the implications of technology for business, e.g. *Fast Company*, *Business 2.0*. Publications that describe emerging technologies, particularly from an investment perspective, such as *Red Herring* and *Industry Standard*, are also

quite popular. Finally, there are magazines that address more technical issues or how to manage technical projects and teams. *CIO* and *Managing Information Strategies* are good starting points for this type of information. This book should have provided the foundation knowledge necessary to interpret most of the information contained in any of these publications. Also, talk to your IT department. For many business leaders and senior management we realize that this is a fate worse than death! Yet, in our years in research and advising businesses, we can point consistently to the relationship between business and IT managers as one of the major influences determining the successful use of technology in companies.

3. Continually re-evaluate what technology can do for your business. This must be done for at least two reasons. First, new technologies are constantly emerging that make possible entirely new business models or applications. Second, due to the decreasing price (and increasing capabilities) of IT, many applications that had a negative ROI or business case last year may have a positive ROI this year. This is often the area where business leaders can have the most impact on their company. Many IT professionals lack the strategic insight necessary to redesign major aspects of the business or develop entirely new technology-enabled business strategies. At the same time, business leaders often lack the understanding of the capabilities of IT to determine what is feasible. In most cases, many of these opportunities must be pursued with multi-disciplinary teams, involving both business and IT professionals, in order to capture the depth of knowledge necessary to develop and evaluate potential business transformation fully. We hope this book will provide leaders with the technical courage to pursue the wealth of technology inspired business opportunities awaiting them, and even more importantly with the courage to engage IT professionals in meaningful conversation while not drowning in an ocean of terminology and acronyms.

Appendix I:
Glossary of IT acronyms

Term	Stands For	Means	Category
3DES	Triple Data Encryption Standard	A methodology using the DES security algorithm three times in a row, in order to increase security	Security
3G	Third Generation (mobile telephony)	Alternative word for UMTS – a standard for global mobile telephony supporting much higher data rates – up to 2 Mbps	Wireless Telephony
3GL	Third Generation language	Name applied to imperative/functional programming languages like Cobol, Basic, and C	Development
4G	Fourth Generation (mobile telephony)	Extension of 3G networks, so that fixed portion of wireless network is entirely IP-based	Wireless Telephony
4GL	Fourth Generation language	Name applied to languages that are closer to human languages than 3GLs. Often database access languages are called 4GLs	Development
802.11x	IEEE802.11/a/b/g	A number of standards for Wireless Local Area Networking. 802.11 was a 1–2 Mbps standard, 802.11b is 11 Mbps, 802.11a is 54 Mbps.	Wireless LAN
ADO	ActiveX Database Objects	A Microsoft technology for database access	Development
ADSL	Asynchronous Digital Subscriber Line	A high-speed communications protocol, primarily aimed at the home market, compelling because it works over traditional telephony infrastructure	Communications
AES	Advanced Encryption Standard	An encryption standard, chosen to replace DES	Security
AI	Artificial Intelligence	Any formula or approach that has some element of learning, or advanced predictive or decision-making behaviour that seems to produce 'human-like' outputs	Development

Term	Stands For	Means	Category
AMPS	Analog Mobile Phone System	A US standard for analog mobile phones, a predecessor to digital mobile phones, but still quite popular	Wireless Telephony
ANSI	American National Standards Institute	US technical standards body	Organization
AOA	Angle of Arrival	A method of calculating location of a mobile handset based on the angle that waves sent from it arrive at a base station	Mobile Internet
AP	Access Point	In Wireless LAN the AP provides the bridge to the wired network	Wireless LAN
API	Application Programming Interface	The interface defined for working with a third party program or library	Development
ARPU	Average Revenue Per User	Term used in telecoms for monthly revenue from consumers	Wireless Telephony
ASCII	American Standard Code for Information Interchange	A code for mapping the alphabet into binary bytes. The most popular way for storing characters. (e.g. 65 decimal = 'A', 97 decimal = 'a')	Other
ASIC	Application Specific Integrated Circuit	A CPU-like chip that is custom designed for a specific application/environment, with circuitry that relates to that specific environment	Chips
ASP (I)	Active Server Pages	A Microsoft technology for creating Web interfaces that are linked to back-end server programs (rather than just static HTML Web pages)	Web
ASP (II)	Application Service Provider	New business model, where IT solutions are deployed outside the corporation, and rented to the corporation	Business Model
ATA	Advanced Technology Attachment	ANSI's name for the IDE bus	Storage
ATM	Asynchronous Transfer Mode	Comms standard for wide area transmission	Communications
Baud	Baud	A measure of signal speed, similar to bits-per-second. For technical reasons, baud is not exactly the same as bps – not very important measure now	Units
BCD	Binary Coded Decimal	Way of storing decimal numbers in binary bytes	Other
BIOS	Basic Input Output System	Kernel of a computer's operating system that manages basic interactions with peripherals attached to the computer's buses	Firmware

Term	Stands For	Means	Category
BLEC	Building Local Exchange Carrier	A term coined for those providing wireless access to the Internet in buildings/public spaces, e.g. Mobilestar	Wireless LAN
Bluetooth	Bluetooth	A standard for ad-hoc wireless networking, originally created by Ericsson	Wireless LAN
BORE	Break Once Run Everywhere	The concept that, once a program has been hacked, it can be freely distributed by hackers	Security
BSI	British Standards Institute	A UK institution which defines standards including IT standards	Organization
CASE	Computer Aided Software Engineering	Methodology for designing software applications using computer tools	Development
CCITT	Consultative Committee for International Telegraph & Telephone	A technology and telecomms standards organization	Organization
CDMA	Code Division Multiple Access	A digital mobile telephony standard, mostly used in the US	Wireless Telephony
CDMA2000	Code Division Multiple Access 2000	New version of CDMA used as Basis for UMTS, along with WCDMA	Wireless Telephony
CDN	Content Distribution Networks	An emerging sub-industry/methodology for 'caching' rich Internet content in many places around the Internet to increase speed. Akamai are a key player	Web
CDPD	Cellular Packet Digital Data	A wireless data standard used by pager networks in the Americas	Wireless Telephony
CD-R/CD-RW	Compact Disc-Recordable, -Read Write	A compact disc used as a computer storage medium. Each piece of a CD-R disc is writable once, whereas CD-RW are writable many times. Even CD-RW wear out eventually	Storage
CGA	Colour Graphics Adapter	Old standard for PC video output	Hardware
CGI	Common Gateway Interface	Standard approach to linking Web pages to server programs	Web
CGMP	General Conference on Weights and Measures (French)	French organization responsible for standardizing terms such as Tera, Peta	Organization
cHTML (I)	Compact HTML	Subset of HTML used for i-Mode	Web, Mobile Internet
cHTML (II)	Compiled HTML	Compressed form of HTML used for help files	Web

Term	Stands For	Means	Category
CIO	Chief Information Officer	Normally the most senior member of the IT department in a non-IT company – c.f. CTO	IT Roles
CISC	Complex Instruction Set Computer	Term for a standard CPU (e.g. Intel Pentium) compared with a reduced instruction set chip (RISC) which purports to run faster through simpler, faster machine code	Chips
CLEC	Competitive Local Exchange Carrier	A term for local phone companies, particularly in the US	Telephony
COM	Component Object Model	Microsoft technology for run-time object communications	Development
CORBA	Common Object Request Broker Architecture	A standard for allowing programs to be distributed over several servers, and to synchronize/share data with each other	Development, Object Orientation
CPM	Cost Per Thousand	Advertising term, used to define how much an advertiser pays for 1 thousand views of their advert	Units
CPU	Central Processing Unit	The chip that is the heart of the computer. One example is the Intel Pentium III	Chips
CRM	Customer Relationship Management	A class of software designed to help with serving and understanding customers	Software
CSS	Cascading Style Sheet	A means of personalizing Web page formatting, expected to be superseded by XSL	Web
CTO	Chief Technology Officer	Normally the head of technology in an IT-centric business, cf CIO	IT Roles
DAMPS	Digital AMPS	A digital mobile telephony standard, mostly used in the US, to supersede AMPS	Wireless Telephony
DAT	Digital Audio Tape	A standard for recording and recovering a digital signal from a tape	Storage
DBA	Database Administrator	Role within IT department – takes care of databases	IT Roles, Storage
DCOM	Distributed Component Object Model	Microsoft extension of COM, allowing real-time communications between objects on remote computers	Development
DECT	Digital Enhanced Cordless Telecomms	A standard for cordless telephony	Wireless LAN
DES	Data Encryption Standard	A symmetric encryption standard, using 56-bit keys, which was the preferred standard by the US Department of Defense – not considered very strong any more, and will be replaced by AES	Security

Term	Stands For	Means	Category
DHCP	Dynamic Host Configuration Protocol	Protocol used to assign IP addresses to nodes on LAN	Internet
DIMM	Dual InLine Memory Module	A circuit board containing several memory chips, a double SIMM	PC Hardware
DLL	Dynamic Linked Library	A library of software functions that is loaded into memory on a Microsoft operating system, in order to provide 'helper' functions to programs	Development
DLT	Digital Linear Tape	A standard tape format for data usage	Storage
DNS	Domain Name Service	Service to map Web domains (e.g. www.ibm.com) to IP addresses (e.g. 100.200.12.6)	Internet
DOS	Disk Operating System	Early name for operating system, as this includes file system	Software
DRM	Digital Rights Management	Techniques for enforcing the protection of owners'/licensees' rights over digital content	Security
DSL	Digital Subscriber Line	Family of high speed comms standards for Internet access, e.g. ADSL	Communications
DSLAM	Digital Subscriber Line Access Multiplexer	Equipment that Telcos need to aggregate many DSL connections	Communications
DSSS	Direct Sequence Spread Spectrum	Method for spreading data communications over a larger than necessary spectrum, for both confidentiality and robustness. Used by 802.11x standards	Wireless LAN
DTD	Document Type Definition	Component of XML technology set. Used to define the syntax of an XML language, e.g. MathML	Web
DTP	DeskTop Publishing	The ability to work with documents and their format on-screen	Graphics
DVD	Digital Versatile Disk	Standard for data storage – same size disks as CD, but much higher density	Storage
DVR	Digital Video Recorder	Technology for replacing tape-based VCRs with VCRs that use a hard-disk drive to store digitized video	Infotainment
EAI	Enterprise Application Integration	A class of software that helps 'glue' different enterprise applications together	Software
EBCDIC	Extended Binary Code for Data Interchange	IBM standard for text coding, much like ASCII. Incompatible with, and largely superseded by, ASCII and Unicode	Other

Term	Stands For	Means	Category
EDGE	Enhanced Data GSM Environment	Mobile phone data technology offering up to 384 kbps. May not be widely deployed – UMTS/3G offers more	Wireless
EGA	Enhanced Graphics Adapter	Old standard for PC video output (higher resolution than CGA)	PC Hardware
EIDE	Enhanced Integrated Drive Electronics	An improved version of the IDE PC Bus	PC Hardware
EISA	Extended Industry Standard Architecture	Standard for PC cards	PC Hardware
ELSI	Extremely Large Scale Integration	Description of a density of chip technology	Chips
EMS	Enhanced Messaging System	Enhancement to SMS to allow pictures, icons, and ringtones	Mobile Internet
EOTD	(Enhanced) Observed Time of Departure	A method of calculating location of a mobile handset based on the timing of the sending of signals	Location, Mobile Internet
ERP	Enterprise Resource Planning	A class of software designed to automate business processes	Software
Ethernet	Ethernet	Main standard for lower layers of LANs	Network Technologies
ETL	Extract, Transform, Load	A class of tools that help with loading data into a database, typically for data warehousing/mining purposes	Software
ETSI	European Telecommunications Standards Institute	Responsible for a number of wireless and wireless data standards, including HiperLAN	Organization
Exa	Exa	Means 10^{18}. Comes from Greek Hex, meaning six (Kilo^6)	Units
FAQ	Frequently Asked Questions	Often on Websites, a list of answers to commonly asked questions, as a support mechanism	Other
FCIA	Fibre Channel Industry Association	Industry association for fibre channel storage networking	Storage, Organization
FCIP	Fibre Channel Internet Protocol	Method of allowing fibre channel storage to attach to IP networks	Storage
FHSS	Frequency Hopping Spread Spectrum	Method for spreading data communications over a larger than necessary spectrum, for both confidentiality and robustness. Used by older versions of 802.11x standards	Wireless LAN
FLOPS	Floating Point Operations Per Second	Measure of systems performance	Units

Term	Stands For	Means	Category
FTP	File Transfer Protocol	Protocol for managing copying of files from remote systems over the Internet	Internet
GB	Gigabyte	About 1 billion bytes of storage	Units
GGSN	Gateway GPRS Switching Node	Mobile telephony network component that routes IP packets between a GPRS network and other packet networks, such as the Internet	Mobile
Giga	Giga	Means 10^9. Comes from Latin gigas, meaning giant	Units
GMSC	Gateway Mobile Switching Centre	Specialized mobile telephony network component for connecting mobile switching centres (MSCs)	Mobile
GPRS	General Purpose Radio System	A protocol for creating packet-switched data networks on top of GSM voice networks	Wireless Telephony
GPS	Global Positioning System	A system for determining approximate geographic location based on readings from earth-orbiting satellites	Location
GSM	Global System for Mobile communication	Most prevalent mobile telephony standard in the world, with over 500 million subscribers as of 05/2001	Wireless Telephony
GUI	Graphical User Interface	A user interface which supports windows, icons, etc.	Graphics
H323	H323	A protocol for encoding voice over IP data networks	Telephony
HBA	Host Bus Adapter	Term used for connecting devices to shared 'buses', e.g. connecting fibre channel disks to the fibre channel carrier	Storage
HDD	Hard Disk Drive	A hard disk drive to use with a PC	Storage
HDLC	High-speed Data Link Control	A low-level comms protocol, based on IBM SDLC	Communications
HDML	Handheld Device Markup Language	A content description language defined by OpenWave, used as a precursor to WAP in the US, and used as the basis for WML	Mobile Internet
HiperLAN	Hiper Local Area Network	Wireless LAN protocol promoted by ETSI. HiperLAN 1 failed commercially. HiperLAN 2 to compete with 802.11a in 2002–3	Wireless LAN
HLR	Home Location Register	Component in GSM networks that stores information about mobile subscribers	Wireless Telephony
HomeRF	Home Radio Frequency	Wireless LAN standard, specifically designed for home use, low power, and low cost. To be superseded by WBHF (=HomeRF 2)	Wireless LAN

Term	Stands For	Means	Category
HPC	High Performance Computing	Generic term for technologies and initiatives which achieve very high processing throughput	Architecture
HSCSD	High Speed Circuit Switched Data	A method for achieving higher circuit switched data rates from GSM networks, boosting data transfer rates from 9.6 kbps up to a potential maximum of 28.8 kbps	Mobile Internet
HSP	Hosting Service Provider	Name for outsourced hosting provider	Business Model
HTML	HyperText Markup Language	The main standard for describing Web Content	Web
HTTP	HyperText Transfer Protocol	Protocol for managing Web page requests over the Web/Internet	Web
HTTPS	HyperText Transfer Protocol – Secure	A variant of HTTP protocol that has security embedded	Web
ICA	Intermittently Connected Application	Term to describe applications on wireless devices that can operate both with and without Internet connection	Mobile
ICANN	Internet Corporation for Assigned Names and Numbers	An organization responsible for assignment of Web domain names	Organization
ICT	Information and Communications Technology	Broad term for all industries and technologies related to information and communication	Organization
IDE	Integrated Drive Electronics	A PC internal communications bus	PC Hardware
IDE (2)	Integrated Development Environment	A set of tools that facilitate testing and development of software, such as Microsoft Visual Studio	Development
iDTV	Interactive Digital TeleVision	New digital television services that allow significant user interaction	Infotainment
IEEE	Institute of Electrical and Electronic Engineers	A standards body, producing many comms standards (e.g. Ethernet, which is IEEE802.3)	Organization
IEEE1394	IEEE1394	IEEE standard for connecting peripherals to computers. Popular with Apple, Sony, and digital multimedia technology, like cameras. Also called Firewire	Communications
IETF	Internet Engineering Task Force	A regulatory body, related to the Internet	Organization
iFCP	Internet Fibre Channel Protocol	Method of allowing fibre channel storage to attach to IP networks	Storage

Term	Stands For	Means	Category
IIOP	Internet Inter-ORB protocol	A comms protocol used as the transport for communication between Object Request Brokers	Development
IMAP	Internet Message Access Protocol	A protocol for accessing a mail server remotely. A little more powerful than POP3	Internet
i-Mode	i-Mode	Mobile Internet Standard proprietary to Japan's NTT DoCoMo, competitor to WAP	Mobile Internet
IMT2000	International Mobile Telecommunications 2000	3G Telephony standard defined by the International Telecommunication Union	Mobile Internet
Infiniband	Infiniband	Standard for attaching storage to servers at high speed	Storage
IP	Internet Protocol	The protocol that sits on top of TCP (or UDP or other) that allows Internet nodes to identify and send packets to each other	Internet
IP(2) = IPR	Intellectual Property (Rights)	Patents registered with the authorities asserting an organization/individual inventor's rights not to be copied without consent/licensing	Legal
IPS	Instructions per Second	Measure of CPU performance	Units
IPSec	Internet Protocol Security	A security standard for IP traffic that is included as part of IPv6	Internet
IPv6	Internet Protocol Version 6	New version of Internet Protocol (IP), designed to handle more devices	Internet
IR	Infrared	Wireless data connectivity using infrared waves. Different from Radio Frequency (RF) in that devices must be in line-of-sight of each other	Communications
IrDA	Infrared Data Association	Organization and protocol standard for infrared connectivity	Communications
IS	Information Systems	One phrase for describing the IT Department, or the IT industry	Organization
ISA	Industry Standard Architecture	Standard for PC cards	PC Hardware
iSCSI	Internet SCSI	A relatively recent standard, introduced to allow connection of storage devices over the Ethernet/Internet	Storage
ISDN	Integrated Services Digital Network	A high speed WAN protocol, popular in Europe as a premier home connectivity protocol, allowing data rates of up to 128 kbps. Likely to be superseded by ADSL, cable, xDSL.	Communications

Term	Stands For	Means	Category
ISM	Industrial, Scientific and Medical	Global frequency band, intended for industrial, scientific and medical use. Roughly 2.4 Ghz	Wireless
ISO	International Standards Organization	A standards body	Networking
ISP	Internet Service Provider	Provision of Internet connection to businesses/consumers	Business Model
IT	Information Technology	Name for industry involved with digital information processing	Other
ITT	Information Technology & Telecoms	Common aggregation of IT and Telecommunications industries	Other
ITU	International Telecommunications Union	Geneva-based mobile standards body	Organization
IWF	Inter Working Function	Component within a mobile telephony network, interfacing to other mobile networks and fixed networks	Wireless Telephony
J2EE	Java 2 Enterprise Edition	A set of technologies around Java, allowing database access, LDAP directory access, linking to non-Java code, etc.	Development
J2ME	Java 2 Micro Edition	Version of the Java framework that is designed for small devices, e.g. handhelds, home appliances	Development
JAD	Joint Application Development	Technique for rapidly developing applications by involving users at all stages of the development in a joint team	Development
Java	Java	A programming language developed and contributed to the public domain by Sun, particularly suited for Web applications	Development
JavaScript	Java Scripting Language	A language for creating rich I/O experiences within HTML pages. Only very loosely related to Java	Development
JDBC	Java DataBase Connectivity	A Java equivalent of the ODBC standard for vendor-independent database connectivity	Development
JFC	Java Foundation Classes	Program library at the heart of Java, including the Swing GUI library	Development
Jini	Jini	Java 'Spontaneous Networking' standard	Development
JMF	Java Media Framework	Multimedia component of Java J2EE framework	Development

Term	Stands For	Means	Category
JMS	Java Messaging Service	Component of J2EE that provides reliable messaging	Development
JMX	Java Management Extensions	Component of J2EE that provides remote management capabilities	Development
JNDI	Java Native Directory Interface	J2EE component for accessing LDAP directories	Development
JNI	Java Native Interface	J2EE component for interfacing between Java and modules written in other languages, such as C++	Development
JSP	Java Server Pages	Java version of ASP – a technique for creating Web interfaces to server-based programs	Development
JVM	Java Virtual Machine	A software application that executes Java bytecode programs	Development
JXTA	Juxtapose	Java P2P communications protocols	Development
KB	Kilobyte	1024 bytes of storage	Units
Kbps	Kilobits/second	Transmission speed of 1000 bits in a second (= about 125 bytes/s)	Units
KHz	Kilohertz	1000 cycles per second	Units
Kilo	Kilo	Means 10^3. Comes from Greek khiloi, meaning 1000	Units
KVM	K Virtual Machine	A very lightweight Java Virtual Machine from Sun, designed for use in small devices	Development
L2TP	Layer 2 Tunnelling Protocol	Virtual Private Network protocol sponsored by Cisco	Communications
LAN	Local Area Network	A set of computers and/or peripherals that are connected to each other, normally within a building, often using the TCP/IP protocol	Networking
LDAP	Lightweight Directory Access Protocol	Standard for storing and structuring directories of information	Development
LSI	Large Scale Integration	Description of a density of chip technology	Chips
MAN	Metropolitan Area Network	Term for networking multimedia residences/ organizations (normally in order to reduce wiring costs)	Networking
MB	Megabyte	About 1 million bytes of storage	Units
Mbps	Megabits/second	Transmission speed of 1 million bits in a second (= about 125 thousand bytes/s)	Units
Mega	Mega	Means 10^6. Comes from Greek mega, meaning great	Units

Term	Stands For	Means	Category
MFCP	Metropolitan Fibre Channel Protocol	Method of allowing fibre channel storage to attach to IP networks	Storage
MHz	Megahertz	1 million cycles per second, common unit for measuring CPU clock speed	Units
MIDp	Mobile Information Device Profile	Set of functions for implementing Java on a mobile device (J2ME)	Development
MIS	Management Information Systems	A name for the IT department, or subset thereof who focus on infrastructure and apps for senior decision makers in an organization	Organization
MMS	Multimedia Messaging System	Enhancement to SMS and EMS to allow full multimedia delivery, including video clips	Mobile Internet
Mobitex	Mobitex	A wireless data standard used by pager networks in the Americas	Wireless Telephony
MPEG	Motion Picture Expert Group	A standards body responsible for many standards for video and audio encoding, including the MPG movie file and the MP3 music standard	Organization
MPP	Massively Parallel Processing	Computing using many processors/ computers in parallel	Architecture
MSC	Mobile Switching Centre	Switching component within a mobile telephony network	Wireless Telephony
MSP	Managed Service Provider	Business model where provider manages clients IT service remotely	Business Model
MT	Machine Translation	Use of computers to translate between natural languages such as English and Japanese	Other
MVNO	Mobile Virtual Network Operator	A wireless operator (such as Virgin in UK, Debitel in Germany) who does not own its own infrastructure, but leases capacity from a network operator, and specializes in customer relationships	Business Model
NAN	Neighbourhood Area Network	Term for non-profit groups putting up WLAN access points in neighbourhoods facilitating wireless Internet access	Wireless LAN
NAS	Network Attached Storage	A thin-server storage mechanism, where a stripped down server serves storage to the LAN, giving higher reliability and reduced cost of ownership	Storage
NAT	Network Address Translation	A mechanism for mapping many IP addresses in a LAN to a few on the Internet, to allow more flexibility within the enterprise	Internet
NUMA	Non-Uniform Memory Access	A class of architectures for parallel processing	Architecture

Term	Stands For	Means	Category
ODB	Object DataBase	A database designed to storage objected-oriented information	Database
ODBC	Open DataBase Connectivity	An API for accessing databases from within high-level language programs such as C++, Java	Development
ODM	Original Design Manufacturer	Business model where branded player designs key product features, then outsources detailed design and manufacture to third party (cf OEM)	Business Model
OEM	Original Equipment Manufacturer	Business model where branded player takes product produced by another company and (re)brands it (cf ODM)	Business Model
OFDM	Orthogonal Frequency Division Multiplexng	A method for encoding data on a radio signal, used in 802.11a, and contender for 802.11g. More efficient than DSSS and FHSS	Wireless LAN
OLAP	OnLine Analytic Processing	Data mining technology, for slicing and dicing multi-dimensional data	Database
OLE	Object Linking and Embedding	Methods of creating run-time links between objects and applications of different types in Microsoft environments	Development
OMA	Open Mobile Alliance	The new name for the WAP Forum, a standards body for mobile data	Organization
ORB	Object Request Broker	An agent that sits on each server, allowing the distribution of software objects transparently across multiple machines	Development
OS	Operating System	Underlying program running on computers, e.g. Windows, Linux	Software
OSI	Open Systems Interconnect	A seven-layer theoretical model for networking, developed by ISO	Networking
PAN	Personal Area Network	Term for an ad-hoc personal network, formed from all the devices around the user. Bluetooth PAN is called Piconet	Wireless LAN
PB	Pedabyte/Petabyte	About 1000 trillion bytes of storage	Units
PBCC	Packet Binary Convolutional Codes	A method for encoding data on a radio signal, contender for 802.11g	Wireless LAN
PCI	Peripheral Component Interconnect	A standard for PC cards	PC Hardware
PCMCIA	Personal Computer Memory Card International Association	Standard for laptop plug-in cards. Defines physical and electrical characteristics	PC Hardware
PDA	Personal Digital Assistant	A mobile electronic device that performs personal information management (calendar, address list etc.) and other functions	Mobile

Term	Stands For	Means	Category
PDC	Personal Data Cellular	Mobile telephony standard, used in Japan	Wireless Telephony
PDC-P	Personal Data Cellular – Packet	Extension to Japanese PDC telephony standard, allowing for packet data (as GPRS will extend GSM)	Wireless Telephony
PDF	Portable Document Format	Adobe standard for sharing documents containing text and graphics	File formats
Peta	Peta	Means 10^{15}. Comes from Greek Pente, meaning five (Kilo^5)	Units
PGP	Pretty Good Privacy	A public key encryption product	Security
PHS	Personal Handyphone System	Japanese system for mobile phones within metropolitan areas	Wireless
Piconet	Piconet	Term for a Bluetooth ad-hoc network, formed from all the devices around the user. Equivalent to a PAN	Networking
PIM	Personal Information Management	General term for applications that manage address books, diaries, email and other personal information	Other
PKI	Public Key Infrastructure	An encryption method that is extremely powerful since knowing how to encrypt does not help you decrypt – becoming widely used on the Internet	Security
POP3	Post Office Protocol 3	A protocol for accessing a mail server remotely. A little less powerful than IMAP	Internet
POTS	Plain Old Telephone System	Term used for the use of standard telephone lines, to differentiate from ADSL, cable, etc.	Communications
PPP	Point to Point Protocol	Protocol for managing Internet sessions over serial line (e.g. telephone) connections	Communications
PPTP	Point to Point Tunnelling Protocol	Virtual private network protocol sponsored by Microsoft and others	Communications
PVR	Personal Video Recorder	A set-top box that uses digital video recorder (DVR) technology to provide advanced video recorder capabilities	Infotainment
RAD	Rapid Applications Development	Programming methodology, involving incremental development, such that end results can be viewed often, almost like continuously prototyping	Development
RADSL	Rate Adaptive Digital Subscriber Line	Form of Digital Subscriber Line that changes speed based on quality and distance of connection	Communications
RAID	Redundant Array of Inexpensive Disks	A series of standards for using several smaller disks to provide a faster, more reliable virtual disk through striping and mirroring	Storage

Term	Stands For	Means	Category
RAM	Random Access Memory	General purpose memory chips, that are both readable and writable	Chips
RAS	Remote Access Server	A bank of modems located at an ISP/corporate allowing modem access from home/branch office users	Networking
RDBMS	Relational Database Management System	Dominant architecture for organizing databases, with data stored in tables	Database
RDO	Remote Data Objects	A Microsoft standard for database access	Development
RF	Radio Frequency	Wireless data connectivity using radio waves. Many different standards (e.g. DSSS, FHSS) for encoding data on RF	Wireless LAN
RISC	Reduced Instruction Set Computer	Term for a chip architecture designed to run faster through simpler, faster machine code	Chips
ROM	Read Only Memory	Memory chips that are only readable, not changeable	Chips
RPC	Remote Procedure Call	Distributed computing technology, allowing procedures to invoke each other on different machines	Development
SAN	Storage Area Networks	Technologies for attaching servers and intelligent disks together for shared, high-speed storage – often use fibre channel communications	Storage
SAS	Server Attached Storage	Conventional disk storage, where disks are attached directly to the server/client computer, using technologies such as SCSI	Storage
SCSI	Small Computer Systems Interface	A standard for connecting computers to storage devices and other peripherals	Storage
SDK	Software Development Kit	A set of software libraries with well defined APIs, documentation, and support capabilities to allow programmers to develop applications	Development
SDLC	Synchronous Data Link Control	An IBM low-level comms protocol, commonly used for communication with mainframe computers	Communications
SDR	Software Defined Radio	Systems that use software to modulate and demodulate radio signals (as opposed to having it hardcoded)	Wireless
SDSL	Synchronous Digital Subscriber Loop	Fast DSL technology that provides equal bandwidth outbound and inbound (unlike ADSL)	Communications
SET	Secure Electronic Trading	A secure e-commerce standard developed by Visa, Mastercard, Microsoft, Netscape, including digital wallets	Security

Term	Stands For	Means	Category
SGML	Standard Generalized Markup Language	A very comprehensive 'markup language', for describing structured data. XML is a simplified version of SGML	Web
SGSN	Serving GPRS Support Node	Mobile telephony network component that passes IP packets to/from handsets and a GPRS network	Mobile
SIM	Subscriber Identity Module	Smart card that goes inside a phone/WID, holding user's identity and some programs	Wireless Telephony
SIMM	Single Inline Memory Module	A circuit board containing several memory chips	PC Hardware
SIP	Session Initiation Protocol	A protocol defined by IETF for managing multimedia (voice, video, data) sessions	Telephony
SLA	Service Level Agreement	Contract made with outsourcing provider to guarantee level of service	Legal
SLIP	Serial Line Internet Protocol	Protocol for managing Internet sessions over serial line (e.g. telephone) connections	Communications
SMP	Symmetric Multiprocessing	An approach for parallel processing where multiple processors share the same memory space	Architecture
SMS	Short Message Service	Technology for sending text messages to/from mobile phones on GSM networks using the signalling channel, SS7	Mobile Internet
SMTP	Simple Mail Transfer Protocol	Protocol for mail servers to communicate with each other to facilitate the sending and receiving of e-mail	Internet
SNIA	Storage Networking Industry Association	Industry association for fibre channel storage networking	Storage
SOAP	Simple Object Access Protocol	Microsoft-originated standard for passing data between programs, based on XML	Development
SQL	Structured Query Language	A standard language for accessing relational database information, supported by most RDBMS	Database
SS7	Signalling System 7	Signalling channel on GSM networks, also used for SMS	Wireless Telephony
SSL	Secure Sockets Layer	A Web protocol for maintaining security through encryption. To be superseded by TLS	Web, Security
SSP	Storage Service Provider	Business model where provider makes storage available over the Internet/leased line	Business Model

Term	Stands For	Means	Category
STB	Set Top Box	Term for a number of new devices, aimed at the home, that provide services such as interactive digital TV, or hard-disk video recording	Infotainment
SVGA	Super Video Graphics Array	Standard for PC video output – higher resolution than VGA	PC Hardware
SWAP	Shared Wireless Access Protocol	Protocol used by DECT and HomeRF	Wireless LAN
TAPI	Telephony Application Programming Interface	A standard application programming interface (API) for telephony applications	Development
TB	Terabyte	About 1 trillion bytes of storage	Units
TCP/IP	Transmission Control Protocol/Internet Protocol	Most common protocol used for LANs; roughly corresponding to layers 3 and 4 of the OSI model	Internet
TCPA	Trusted Computing Platform Alliance	Group designing a more secure PC platform, formed by Compaq, HP, IBM, Intel, and Microsoft	Security
TDMA	Time Division Multiple Access	A digital mobile telephony standard, mostly used in the US	Wireless Telephony
TDOA	Time Difference of Arrival	A method of calculating location of a mobile handset based on the time for waves sent from it to arrive at a base station	Mobile Internet
Tera	Tera	Means 10^{12}. Comes from Greek Teras, meaning monster	Units
TLS	Transport Layer Security	A standard for security that supersedes SSL	Web, Security
TMT	Telecoms, Media & Technology	A collective name for these three industries, which is sometimes used to group individuals/teams in financial institutions based on similar industry dynamics	Organization
TOSR	Trusted Operating System Root	The unhackable core of the PC that is part of Microsoft's Palladium initiative	Security
TPC	Transaction processing Performance Council	An organization that manages a set of benchmarks for online transaction processing performance	Organization
TPM	Trusted Platform Module	The unhackable core of the PC that is the vision of the TCPA	Security
TPS	Transactions per second	A measure of speed of a hardware or software system	Units

Term	Stands For	Means	Category
UDDI	Universal Description, Discovery and Integration	.NET protocol for looking up Web services	Web
UDP	User Datagram Protocol	An alternative to TCP for the network layer of a networking stack, suited to real time applications such as streaming, since if packets are missed they are ignored	Communications
UML	Unified Modelling Language	Formal approach to designing object oriented software	Development
UMTS	Universal Mobile Telephony System	Mobile telephony standard, expected to be available globally in 2003–2004, that allows for data rates up to 2 Mbps	Wireless Telephony
Unicode	Universal Code	A standard for text coding, designed to supersede ASCII/EBCDIC, and to include alphabets from all countries, including China and Japan	Other
URL/URI	Universal Resource Locator/Identifier	Term for the way of defining the location of a file or other object on the Internet, e.g. www.ibm.com/index.html	Web
UWB	Ultra Wide Band	Currently experimental WLAN protocol allowing up to 60 Mbps	Wireless LAN
V90	V90	56 kbps modem standard	Communications
VCR	Video Cassette Recorder	Conventional tape-based video recorder	Infotainment
VDSL	Very high speed DSL	High-speed variant of Digital Subscriber Line technology	Communications
VGA	Video Graphics Array	Standard for PC video output – higher resolution than EGA	PC Hardware
VLR	Visitor Location Register	Holds information from the HLR for users in a specific geographical area	Wireless Telephony
VLSI	Very Large Scale Integration	Description of a density of chip technology	Chips
VOIP	Voice Over Internet Protocol	The carrying of voice traffic over IP data networks	Internet
VPN	Virtual Private Network	A method for creating a secure private communications 'tunnel' through a public medium, i.e. the Internet, using security/encryption	Internet
VR	Virtual Reality	User interface which simulates a 3D world	Graphics
W3C	World Wide Web Committee	A regulatory body, related to the World Wide Web	Organization

Term	Stands For	Means	Category
WAN	Wide Area Network	Linking of two or more local area networks (LANs) using a wide area protocol, such as ISDN or T1	Networking
WAP	Wireless Applications Protocol	A standard for Internet-like functionality over mobile phone networks	Mobile Internet
WASP	Wireless Application Service Provider	Application service provider that is focused on wireless devices	Business Model, Mobile Internet
WBFH	Wide Band Frequency Hopping	New version of home RF wireless LAN protocol	Wireless LAN
WCDMA	Wideband Code Divison Multiple Access	New version of CDMA used as Basis for UMTS, along with CDMA2000	Wireless Telephony
WECA	Wireless Ethernet Compatibility Alliance	A wireless LAN forum, promoter of WiFi	Wireless LAN
WEP	Wired Equivalent Privacy	Security standard component of 802.11	Wireless LAN
WID	Wireless Information Device	Term for next-generation devices that include both data and voice capabilities, similar to Nokia 9110	Mobile Internet
WiFi	Wireless Fidelity	A brand developed by WECA for 2.4 Ghz 802.11b technology, in order to promote interoperability	Wireless LAN
WIM	WAP Identity Module	Component of WAP architecture that enhances security	Mobile Internet
WIMP	Windows, Icon, Mouse, Pointer	Describes the modern PC graphical user interface	Graphics
WISP	Wireless Internet Service Provider	May mean a WiFi hotspot owner, or an ISP that provides wireless 'last mile' connectivity to clients' premises	Internet
WLAN	Wireless Local Area Network	Wireless LAN in homes, offices, factories, using technologies such as 802.11x, Bluetooth, HomeRF	Wireless LAN
WLANA	Wireless LAN Association	A wireless LAN forum	Wireless LAN
WLIF	Wireless Lan Interoperability Forum	A wireless LAN forum	Wireless LAN
WML	Wireless Markup Language	Content markup language component of WAP	Mobile Internet
WMLScript	Wireless Markup Language Scripting Language	A scripting language that can be embedded within WML pages, much as JavaScript can be embedded within HTML pages	Mobile Internet

Term	Stands For	Means	Category
WORM	Write Once, Read Many	A device, such as CD-R, where a disk may be written to once, but from then on only read (not modified)	Storage
WSDL	Web Services Definition Language	.NET protocol for Web services to describe themselves	Web
WSP	Wireless Session Protocol	The protocol for managing user sessions across the WAP transport	Mobile Internet
WTA	Wireless Telephony Application	Aspect of WAP related to voice/data integration	Mobile Internet
WTAI	Wireless Telephony Applications Interface	Aspect of WAP related to voice/data integration	Mobile Internet
WTLS	Wireless Transport Layer Security	Security mechanism in WAP. Currently incompatible with Web security, but likely to improve soon	Mobile Internet
WTP	Wireless Transport Protocol	Transport layer component of WAP protocol stack	Mobile Internet
WWW	World Wide Web	Set of standards and protocols for providing rich, linked content over the Internet in a standard way	Web
WYSIWYG	What You See Is What You Get	Term for solutions where true format of documents is displayed on screen	Graphics
X25	X25	CCITT Standard for wide area networking communications	Communications
XML	Extensible Markup Language	A language for describing content, more sophisticated than HTML, because content is separated from layout	Web
XP	Extreme Programming	A methodology developed by Kent Beck to boost programming quality and productivity, including 'pair programming', where one programmer looks over the other's shoulder	Development
XSL (T)	Extensible Stylesheet Language (Transformation)	XLS is a language for describing presentation formatting rules to apply to XML in order to display it	Web
xSP	(Any) Service Provider	Generic term for Service Provider business models (e.g. ASP, SSP)	Business Model
Yotta	Yotta	Means 10^{24}. Comes from penultimate letter of Latin alphabet	Units
Zetta	Zetta	Means 10^{21}. Comes from last letter of Latin alphabet	Units

Appendix II:
Network communications speeds

Category	Technology	Max speed (mbps)	Comments
Internet Edge	PSTN/POTS/ V.90	0.056 down, 0.0336 up	Standard dial-up modem
	ISDN	0.128	Two 64k channels
	G.Lite ADSL	1.544 down, 0.512 up	
	ADSL	8 down 1 up	
	SDSL	1.544	
	HDSL	1.544 or 2.048	
	VDSL	1.6, 3.2 or 6.4	
	Cable	3–10 down, 2 up	
Internet Backbone (and WAN)	T1	1.544	N.Am standard = 24 voice channels
	T1C	3.152	N.Am standard = 48 voice channels
	T2	6.132	N.Am standard = 96 voice channels
	T3	44.736	N.Am standard = 672 voice channels
	T4	274.176	N.Am standard = 4032 voice channels
	E1	2.048	Euro standard = 30 voice channels
	E2	8.448	Euro standard = 96 voice channels
	E3	34.368	Euro standard = 480 voice channels
	E4	129.264	Euro standard = 1920 voice channels
	E5	565.148	Euro standard = 7680 voice channels
	J1	1.544	Jpn standard = 24 voice channels
	J2	6.312	Jpn standard = 96 voice channels
	J3	32.064	Jpn standard = 480 voice channels
	J4	97.728	Jpn standard = 1440 voice channels
	J5	400.352	Jpn standard = 5760 voice channels
	OC1	51.44	SONET optical standard
	OC3	155.52	SONET optical standard

Note: N.Am = North American; Euro = European; Jpn = Japanese.

Category	Technology	Max speed (mbps)	Comments
	OC12	622	SONET optical standard
	OC24	1244	SONET optical standard
	OC48	2480	SONET optical standard
	OC96	4976	SONET optical standard
	OC192	9953	SONET optical standard
	OC768	39813	SONET optical standard
LAN	Ethernet	10	
	Fast Ethernet	100	
	Gigabit Ethernet	1,000	
PAN/WLAN	802.11b	11	Also called WiFi
	802.11a/g	54/72	Standard 54, some vendors reach 72
	Bluetooth	0.72	
Cellular	GSM	0.010	
	PDC	0.010	
	HSCSD	0.058	
	GPRS	0.171	
	PDC-P	0.029	Used by i-Mode
	EDGE	0.384	
	IMT-2000	2 indoors/fixed, 0.144 roaming	

Note: N.Am = North American; Euro = European; Jpn = Japanese.

Appendix III:
Commonly used computer languages

Language	Type	Execution	Common usage
ABAP	Object Oriented	Intermediate language	Configuring SAP to fit business processes
C	Procedural/ Functional	Compiled	General purpose applications, including real-time control
C#	Object Oriented	Intermediate language	General purpose applications
C++	Object Oriented	Compiled	General purpose applications
Cobol	Procedural/ Functional	Compiled	General purpose applications
Java	Object Oriented	Intermediate language	General purpose applications
Javascript	Procedural/ Functional	Interpreted	Enhancing Web page interactivity/ richness
Jscript	Procedural/ Functional	Interpreted	Enhancing Web page interactivity/ richness
Lisp	Procedural/ Functional	Interpreted or compiled	Artificial intelligence
Machine Code	Machine Code	Machine code	Device drivers
Pascal	Procedural/ Functional	Compiled	General purpose applications
Perl	Procedural/ Functional	Interpreted (can be compiled)	Web server scripting, system admin tools

Language	Type	Execution	Common Usage
PHP	Object Oriented	Interpreted	Web server scripting
Prolog	Logic	Interpreted or compiled	Artificial intelligence
Python	Object Oriented	Interpreted	Web server scripting
SQL	Database	Interpreted[19]	Database
Visual Basic	Procedural/ Functional	Compiled	Corporate Application Development

---

[19] In many implementations of SQL, the first time a piece of code is executed, it is interpreted, then stored in a semi-compiled format, then each time the same code is executed, the semi-compiled version is used.

Appendix IV:
IT literacy test for managers

Objective

This test allows managers to get a feel for their level of information technology (IT) knowledge. Cover the answers on page 171, and try to answer all 20 questions before looking at the answers.

Questions

Some basics

1. What is the role of the operating system in a computer?
2. What are hubs, switches, and routers for, and what is the difference between them?
3. What is the key difference between C and C++, and why is this important for business?
4. What is the key difference between C++ and Java, and why is this important for business?

IT in business

5. What is the role of an ERP system? Who are the top ERP suppliers?
6. If one key value of IT in business is to increase effectiveness through increasing sales (e.g. through exploiting the online channel), what are the other key sources of value of IT to a business?
7. What is the difference between a CTO, a CIO and an IT Director?

Implementing e-commerce

8. Name all the key hardware, software, and network protocol components needed to make an e-commerce purchase, from a home-based client computer to the business's server computer.
9. What are content distribution networks (CDN), and what is their key business benefit?
10. What role do Layer 5 switches play in e-commerce infrastructure?
11. Why is XML an important technology for successful e-business?

Information security

12. If 'confidentiality of information' is one aspect of information security, what are the five other key aspects?
13. What is a DMZ, and how is it used in an e-business?

Wireless and other leading edge technologies

14. Give three reasons why mobile commerce (e-commerce on mobile platforms) requires different technical and commercial considerations from 'fixed' e-commerce.
15. What does the term xInternet refer to, and what is its business value?
16. What are the two major benefits of GPRS mobile technology over GSM?

Bleeding edge technologies

17. What is quantum cryptography, and why will it be important?

IT industry knowledge

18. How large was the global information and communications technology industry, in terms of revenues, in 1999?
    (a) US$250 billion
    (b) US$1 trillion
    (c) US$2 trillion
    (d) US$5 trillion
19. Who are Transmeta, what is their Crusoe product, and why is it important?
20. Who are Akamai, and what is the business value of the service they provide?

Answers

1. The operating system (such as Windows XP™ or Unix) provides services to programs and the end-user, including a graphical user interface (GUI), the file system, and 'drivers' which allow easy usage of disk drives, screen, printers, modem, and other peripherals.

2. Hubs, switches, and routers comprise the plumbing of a local area network. Hubs provide no intelligence, but simply replicate packets of information. Switches provide filtering to reduce traffic. Routers provide an interface from the LAN to wide area networking protocols, to allow connection to a WAN or the Internet.

3. C++ introduces the concept of 'object orientation', allowing programs to be object-based models of the real world problems they are trying to solve, typically increasing reliability and flexibility, and reducing maintenance effort.

4. Java introduced the concept of an intermediate language, allowing programs to be downloaded to client computers over the Internet, and run without compatibility problems.

5. An ERP – or Enterprise Resource Planning – system is used to automate and integrate all the processes across a business, including inventory management, manufacturing, finance and accounting, purchasing etc. The leading players include SAP, Peoplesoft, Baan, and Oracle.

6. Increasing efficiency (through reducing costs, e.g. with process automation), improving communication and collaboration (e.g. through B2B marketplaces), and enhancing learning (e.g. through data mining.)

7. Typically:
    - a CTO manages the IT function and IT strategy in an IT business (i.e. a business whose major products are IT products).
    - A CIO manages the IT function in a business whose main product is non-technical).
    - An IT Director is a more traditional name for either a CIO or a CTO.

8. HARDWARE: Home-based PC -> Modem -> client's ISP's RAS server -> client ISP's routers, firewalls, Domain Name Servers -> business's ISP -> business's router -> business's server computer.
    SOFTWARE: Client's Web browser, business's Web server and e-commerce server software, payment services.
    NETWORK PROTOCOLS: HTTP, HTTPS running over TCP/IP + wide area protocols (e.g. ADSL).

9. Content distribution networks are primarily a means to distribute high band-width Internet content (e.g. streaming video/audio) around the Internet, and direct customers intelligently to the closest site. This increases the quality of the online customer experience.

10. Layer 5 switches are Internet load-balancing switches, allowing Web requests to be farmed out across multiple servers to provide scalability and resilience.

11. XML allows content to be stored in one format for programmatic and user purposes, reducing information errors. It also allows content and presentation to be separated, facilitating presentation of the same content on multiple devices and personalized for different users.

12. Other than confidentiality (message is secret), the aspects of information security are: privacy (who you are talking to is private), integrity (messages can be guaranteed complete and untampered with), authentication (identity of participants can be guaranteed), non-repudiation (neither party can deny a transaction), availability (unauthorized parties cannot cause service to be denied).

13. DMZ stands for demilitarized zone. In general, a corporate firewall should segregate the electronic world into three: an intranet (a controlled, trusted network), the Internet (an uncontrolled, untrusted network), and the DMZ, where the corporate Website is situated, which allows outside users in (unlike the corporate intranet).

14. Differences between m-commerce and e-commerce: wider audience, more personal device, device always with you, greater sociodemographic spread of audience, less standard technology environment, number of powerful oligo-polies in supply chain, walled gardens, more limited devices (processing power, storage, battery life, display, keyboard), security holes, slower and less reliable connectivity, pull modality only (in GSM/CDMA context before packet data).

15. xInternet is the term some analysts are applying to the next generation of Internet software and service technologies which vastly improve on a simple, unpersonalized browser-based experience. 'Web services' is another name for the same thing. Offerings in this space include Microsoft's .NET framework.

16. GPRS, or General Packet Radio Service, offers faster data rates than GSM (up to 115 kbps rather than 9.6 kbps), and also offers 'always on' connectivity, which allows Internet access without waiting for a dialup, and also allows information to be 'pushed' to mobile devices.

17. Quantum cryptography is a technique for massively improving privacy and confidentiality of messages through use of quantum physics principles, ren-dering it impossible to intercept messages passively.

18. (C) – Global ICT revenues were around US$2 trillion in 1999.

19. Transmeta produce the Crusoe chip, which can emulate an Intel chip using a much smaller number of transistors, through an intermediate software layer, making for much less battery consumption, and leaving the possibility of intelligent tuning open. Many laptop manufacturers, such as Sony and Toshiba, have begun using the Transmeta in their laptops.

20. Akamai are a leading Content Distribution Networks provider. Use of their services increases the quality of user experience for their clients, and reduces their e-commerce infrastructure costs.

Appendix V:
Some useful books

Category	Title	Author	Publication details
IT and Information Management Primers	How Computers Work	White	0789725495, Que
	How the Internet Works	Gralla	0789725827, Que
	How Networks Work	Freed & Derfler	0789727536, Que
	Essentials of Management Information Systems	Loudon & Loudon	0130087343, Prentice Hall
	Internet Future Strategies	Amor	013041803X, Prentice Hall
Effects of IT on Industry	Information Rules	Shapiro & Varian	087584863X, Harvard Business School Press
	Blown to Bits	Evans & Wurster	087584877X, Harvard Business School Press
	Waves of Change: Business Evolution Through Information Technology	McKenney	0875845649, Harvard Business School Press
Visioning and The Future of IT	The Invisible Computer	Norman	0262640414, MIT Press
	Being Digital	Negroponte	0679762906, Vintage Books
	The Age of Spiritual Machines	Kurzweil	0140282025, Penguin
	What Will Be	Dertouzos & Gates	0062515403, HarperBusiness
	108 Tips for Time Travellers	Cochrane	0752821075, Texere Publishing

Category	Title	Author	Publication details
IT Industry	Crossing the Chasm	Moore & McKenna	0060517123, HarperBusiness
	Inside the Tornado	Moore	0887308244, HarperCollins
	Boo Hoo	Malmsten	0099418371, Arrow Books
Interesting Technology Topics	The Code Book	Singh	0385495323, Anchor Books
	Fuzzy Thinking	Kosko	078688021X, Hyperion
	Weaving the Web	Berners-Lee	006251587X, HarperBusiness

Index

Numbers in **bold** indicate glossary entries